LESSONS
FROM THE SEA

*Stories of the Deadliest Occupation
from a Bering Sea Captain*

Steven R. Smith

Carpenter's Son Publishing

DEDICATION

*This book is dedicated to my beloved wife Lorraine
whose love, patience and support were instrumental in
this book's creation.
Sweetheart, you are a Highliner in so many ways,
and I was blessed beyond measure the day you accepted
my hand in marriage.
I'll love you forever...*

ACKNOWLEDGEMENTS

This book took more years than it should have but not as many as it could have if it weren't for the support of family and friends. I want to especially thank Lorraine for her persistence in encouraging me to finish this book and her careful editing as well as project management. Thank you, Sweetheart! I couldn't have done it without you.

Becoming a Highliner in the ultra competitive commercial fishing industry was only possible because of the great opportunities I was given as a fisherman. In particular, I want to express my gratitude to David Lethin for entrusting me with his boat and mentoring me through the years. David… you are true leader and one of a kind!

The stories told here were experienced by others, and I want to thank them for allowing me to share them with others. Some of my fondest memories of fishermen include, but are not limited to: Troy (Chief) Huls, Marty McMaster and Curtis Gann.

And above all else, I thank God for His protection and guidance at sea and on land.

FOREWORD

I cannot explain to normal people the suffering and painful lifestyle that a commercial fisherman endures. I have owned four Bering Sea crab boats, several Dungeness crab boats, long line boats and others. I have fished for over 35 years and worked with hundreds of crewmen. In my first year alone, I went through 51 crewmen in 9 months! The author of this book is one of the best fishermen I have ever known during my career. I know because we worked together for 10 years, and Steve never once said no to the task at hand. He quickly earned my respect and admiration and soon took over as Captain of my most prized possession, the fishing vessel Ballad.

Many people who have watched the *Deadliest Catch*® often ask me if it was legal to work these men under the conditions of sleep deprivation, biblical workloads and unimaginable sea conditions. My answer was surprising even to me; I had never reflected from an outsider's point of view looking in. Not once had I wept on the deck of a fishing boat, but telling that story from the outside looking in, I could not help but cry. I can remember one particular season we fished in three hurricane-force storms. The boat was 127 feet long and brand new. I had put another crewman in the wheel house to watch for waves off the port side while I ran the last 40 pots necessary to fill the fish hold and head for town. We would be the first one in fully loaded that season. While still dark, we pulled up to the first buoy before day break and were in a hell of a storm. Waves as big as apartment complexes, cresting to 50 feet, were all around us with some of them dipping over in the distance of the sodium lights. My crew missed the first buoy with the grapple, and I had to turn around stern to the weather and take another pass. At that moment, we took a monster square on the back of the house, caving the stern in eight inches in places. The deck filled with water, and the crew under the forward over-hang stood in waste deep water. Danny, who was the grapple man that morning, waded over to the speaker and asked if this was worth it! I had no response nor could I muster one. That morning as day light broke, we were able to haul all 40 pots and fill the boat. During that couple of hours while hauling gear, seven boats larger than ours had blown all their wheel house windows out. When that happens, all the electronics are ruined and go out the back windows with the waves. Now we had seven vessels within 35 miles of our location with no communication at all. Soon we had C-130 coast guard planes dispatched from Kodiak Island in route to our location to look for the damaged vessels. An 800 foot log ship was also damaged when a wave ripped thousands of 30 foot logs off its deck. Later, I saw that ship, the *Leo Forrest*, in Dutch harbor, and it looked like someone had stuck dozens of 30-foot pretzels all around the freighter's house. Damaged, she was docked for weeks.

So when I answered that question (is it legal to work men under those conditions?) I could not help but cry. I was humbled and saddened by the mere fact of what I had put my crew through for many years.

Highliners will often work 80 hours straight without a nap. Highliners never fish for the money but rather for the competition and that chance to be number one. Often the only recognition for the captain and crew is third hand, walking into a bar and hearing some guys talking about their boat and how much they caught. We all want recognition for what we do in life, that's for sure. This may be the only recognition they ever receive. Captains and crews on Highliners rarely get a pat on the back for a job well done. But they know what they did, and no one or nothing can take that away from them.

These adventures you are about to read are true. They hold incredible lessons for all to gleam, and through these stories, you will see four types of fishermen:

1) Fishermen
2) Commercial Fishermen
3) Professional Fishermen
4) Highliners

Fishermen are a dime a dozen; everyone wants to try it, and most don't make it. Commercial fishermen look at the money and hope to hit the jack pot and get rich. Professional fishermen know one season does not make a career and over time learn how to do it, make money, pay bills, keep the crew happy and make it a lifestyle. Highliners are a different breed; they don't demand respect…they *get* it. They get the best crews, best equipment and will stop at nothing to be number one. Every year, they seem to make the top five percent. They never give up; they work when things break down; they just make things happen when others give up. They aren't just lucky because they consistently produce results over and over again. And at the end of the season, everyone else is asking Highliners how they did because they *are* the bench mark.

Steve Smith is a Highliner, and I am grateful to have worked with him for so many years. Thank you Steve for your loyalty and sacrifice and for bringing these stories to life for so many. What an honor to have you on board!

Capt. David Lethin

PROLOGUE

The men and women of the commercial fishing industry seek their fortunes in a world of extremes. The weather is often brutal, with bitterly cold winds of 50 mph or more driving immense waves the size of two and three story buildings whose spray can coat a vessel with half a foot of solid ice in minutes. The payoff for success can be high and results from almost any action may be immediate and mistakes can be deadly.

In this ultra-competitive, high-risk world of commercial fishing, an elite group of fishermen referred to as the "Highliners" exist. By consistently employing a common set of operating principles, these fishermen are able to consistently produce greater results than their peers; finding success where others meet failure. While this environment is one that most people are likely never to encounter, it provides a unique metaphor for daily living.

Each and every day whether in our business or personal life, we are fishing... casting our nets of influence and expectation into the waters of life for success, happiness, love or acceptance. When reaching for our dreams, we bait our hooks with purpose and (hopefully!) preparation then cast them into the sea of opportunity.

By applying the same operating principles that produce consistent results for a top producing commercial fisherman, indeed the same principles employed by successful corporate executives, entrepreneurs, salesmen, athletes, politicians, policemen, schoolteachers or farmers we can become Highliners in all areas of our lives because they are *foundational* principles upon which everything else we build spiritually, emotionally, socially and financially comes to rest.

In the pages that follow, see through the eyes of a crab fishing Captain and experience the danger, excitement and wonder of a world few ever experience and learn the lessons of the sea.

Deep inside, we all share a common desire to use the God given talents we were born with in a way that will touch the hearts and minds of those around us in a positive and empowering way. I hope and pray that you will learn to incorporate the principles revealed in this book in every aspect of your life, and in doing so, come to understand the unique and wonderful talents that have been entrusted to you. May you invest those talents wisely and share their bountiful harvest with others.

So cast off the lines, turn the page and set sail for a journey on the cold waters of the North Pacific! I wish you fair winds, a following sea and may you be kept safe in the hands of God throughout your voyage and in all those to come.

Steven R. Smith

TABLE OF CONTENTS

SECTION I:

STORMS AT SEA

"Humility must always be the portion of any man who receives acclaim earned in the blood of his followers and the sacrifices of his friends."

~ Dwight D. Eisenhower ~

CHAPTER ONE
Highliners

"Success is not a harbor but a voyage with its own perils to the spirit.
The game of life is to come up a winner, to be a success,
or achieve what we set out to do.
Yet there is always a danger of failing as a human being.
The lesson that most of us on this voyage never learn,
but can never quite forget, is that to win is sometimes to lose."

- Richard M. Nixon -

"We're on a roll! Way to go guys! Let's get while the gettin's good!" I hollered out over the roar of the wind.

The Ballad, a sixty-foot crab fishing boat, lurched as another dark wave crested then slammed into her from the port side with a thunderous impact, cascading tons of icy, whitewater down on the crew and across the deck. Struggling to keep their feet and maintain a grip on the hydraulic equipment as the water surged around them, Marty and Jeff hollered with excitement as the next crab pot broke the surface of the water.

"Yeeeehaw! Check it out! It's stuffed!"

Looking back from the warm confines of the wheelhouse, I laughed as yet another wave shook the boat and tumbled across the deck. The hydraulic winches groaned as my crew hoisted yet another pot, completely and utterly filled with huge, blue-backed ocean run Dungeness crab onboard. In the ten years I participated in this fishery, I never saw such a phenomenal catch. Barely two weeks into the season, and we already delivered over $300,000 worth of crab. My crew was earning close to $1,000 per day, and we had no competition in sight.

Tough Salts

By nature, commercial fishing is an industry of extremes where results may be immediate and unintended consequences can be deadly. The boats that fish the North Pacific vary widely in size from thirty-foot salmon boats to the 150+ foot crab fishers and factory ships plying the cold waters of the Bering Sea. All carry tough, hardened crewmembers who regularly brave fierce storms and bitter cold in pursuit of their catch. The typical work day for a commercial crab fisherman may last twenty hours or more on a heaving, pitching deck where the simple act of standing is almost impossible without something to hold onto. Driven by storm force winds of fifty knots or more, icy waves as high as a two-story house may crash over the deck with such force as to sweep anything in their path over the side. Then, with temperatures plummeting to below freezing, the vessel begins to take on a surrealistic form as the sea spray forms a layer of ice on the hull and the rigging while the crew works on in a relentless cadence sounded out by the ring of steel against steel, and the whine of hydraulic winches. Still no coffee break, the men subsist on candy bars, soda pop and sheer will as again, day turns to night and the darkness closes in.

As we continued to haul pots that were bursting with crab aboard, I thought back to a dark lonely night in the early days of my fishing career, and we were at the end of another sleepless, brutally cold Alaskan king crab fishing season known to be one of the most dangerous and physically demanding jobs in the world. From the back deck of the eighty-foot trawler Miss Donna, I stood looking over at the giant crab boat tied alongside, shaking my head in amazement. What a beautiful boat, all painted up and sitting proud! Over 100 feet long, the Shaman was consistently one of the top producing crabbers in the fleet. How was it that they always seemed to catch so much more than anyone else was? What did they do that set them apart from the rest? What was the secret that made them…?

Highliners

"…Highliners. That's what'cha call fishermen and boats that always catch more than anybody else does," Jeff replied, stuffing his hands deep into the pockets of his Levi's. "Seems like year in and year out it's always the same guys, too…"

"Well what're they doing?" I asked, "Let's copy 'em!"

Jeff laughed, "On this ol' boat? Yeah right! Best we could do is try to get a job on a boat that's already a Highliner, but you gotta know Captains to get a job."

I was in my first semester attending the Bering Sea School of Hard Knocks and like any greenhorn, I was full of grand ideas and simple answers. Accompanied by the quiet hum of electrical generators aboard the collection of fishing boats tied to the dock, we sat under the bright stars on that cold Arctic night, our breathe glistening as our voices melted into the quiet. We daydreamed of the time when we might be lucky enough to work on a boat like the Shaman, a day when we, too, might be considered Highliners. I asked all kinds of questions, and Jeff provided answers to the myriad of topics that seemed important for a young fisherman to know at the time. I learned that leaving port on a Friday was bad luck and so was painting a boat green because it would then want to turn towards land. Re-naming a boat was bad luck as was leaving a hatch upside down because doing so would cause the boat to turn over to match the hatch. Having women, plants, or cats on board all caused bad luck. "And whatever ya do, don't whistle in the wheelhouse, or you'll whistle up a storm!" No wonder being a Highliner was so tough with all that bad luck to watch out for!

"Accomplishment will always prove to be a journey, not a destination."

~Dwight D. Eisenhower~

Now, 14 years later looking back at my crew as they hauled pot after pot aboard the Ballad, I began to recognize how far I had come from the misinformation and excuses of those early days. I worked my way up through the ranks of the commercial fishing industry on the cold and stormy waters of the North Pacific Ocean and Bering Sea, first as a crewmember, then engineer, and now as Captain. I fished the blue waters of northern California, Oregon, and Washington, on up through the storm tossed Gulf of Alaska, Aleutian Islands, and the bitter cold of the Bering Sea. Earning my degree in the "Bering Sea School of Hard Knocks", my professors included bitter, hardened men struggling to make a living and polished businessmen building multi-million dollar empires. The boats they skippered doubled as classrooms, teaching patience and flexibility. The sea taught me the importance of faith, and in its power, humility. Along the way, I learned a common set of operating principles that were consistently employed by the fishermen who were counted among the best of the best, and as yet another pot surfaced, bulging at the seams with Dungeness crab, I realized that not only had I taken those principles to heart, I made them my own. Three weeks into the season, having landed almost a quarter of a million pounds of Dungeness crab, we were on a record setting pace. We were Highliners!

Break!

Suddenly, the hair on the back of my neck stood on end. Looking out toward the wide-open expanse of the Pacific Ocean, I saw a mountain of dark blue water capped with a thin, white line of froth as the huge wave, its journey of a thousand miles almost at an end as it began its slide up into the shallower water near the beach, begin to collapse upon itself. "This can't be!" my mind screamed, "It can't be cresting that far off-shore. Not in almost 100 feet of water!" But countless tons of water moving ashore quietly, relentlessly, with the power to destroy virtually anything in its path, was bearing down on the Ballad as we turned to face the onslaught in only thirty feet of water beneath our keel. At that depth, this wave would almost certainly top forty feet in height with the top fifteen feet most likely presenting itself as a fifteen-foot wall of curling, foaming, angry whitewater. Facing a wave this size in water this shallow, the possibility existed that the boat could be thrown sideways and rolled over like a pop can with all gear, equipment, and crew aboard cast into turbulence of forty-five degree water that was sure to follow. Images of shattering glass and men struggling for their lives in the icy water amidst the bent and broken rigging of an overturned fishing boat flooded my mind.

"C'mon, break, break!" I muttered, turning the boat straight offshore to face the wave head-on, as though through sheer force of will I could influence the wave to expend its enormous energy and collapse upon itself before it reached the *Ballad*.

"Guys! Big wave coming! Get under the shelter and hang on. And I mean hang on!" I hollered over the intercom. We had no place to hide, nothing to do but wait for the impact of hundreds of tons of icy, crushing water that was sure to follow. Memories of past fishing trips flashed through my mind as the Ballad rested almost peacefully, bow facing the open sea that we crossed so many times earlier that season, a season that up until now had been one of our best ever. Now it seemed it would all end under the terrible, crushing weight of hundreds of tons of icy, crushing water...

CHAPTER TWO
Setting Course

"Luck is a matter of preparation meeting opportunity."

-Oprah Winfrey-

A month before I was muttering to myself while squinting through a rain-spattered windshield. I could see my "home away from home" the Shilo Inn looming out of the gray clouds and sheets of rain that seemed to perpetually blanket the towns of Astoria and Warrenton. Here in the northwest corner of Oregon, the Columbia River empties itself into the North Pacific Ocean. Prior to being tamed with countless hydroelectric dams and its treacherous channels subdued through dredging, navigational beacons and sea walls, the once mighty Columbia poured into the sea with such a ferocity that the resulting tidal currents, sand bars and harsh winter weather earned it the name, "Graveyard of the Pacific." But today, as I crossed the Young's Bay Bridge, it just looked cold, gray, and dreary with wisps of fog blowing through the trees that lined the shores of the river.

Season Opener

The Dungeness crab season was delayed a month due to a strike by the fishing fleet. The canneries balked at first to the higher price asked for by the fishermen, but after several weeks of negotiating, a price settlement appeared imminent. With the late start, we wouldn't have the usual 72-hour "dump time" before the season that allowed all of the boats to get their crab pots baited and set it in neat rows on the flat sandy bottom that ran parallel to the beach just north of the mouth of the Columbia River.

Instead, the season opener promised to be a madhouse of activity as an endless line of fishing boats would steam past the lighthouse atop the dark cliffs of Cape Disappointment, between the twin rock jetties, and across the huge swells that are produced as the Columbia River empties it's millions of gallons of water across the shifting sandbars, marking the mouth of the mighty river as it flows headlong into the sea beyond. In the coming days, the river bar would soon come to resemble Grand Central Station far more than any "Graveyard," as the crabbers scrambled out to sea in a hurry to set the pots that were stacked high on their decks, and then return for more. This scene would be played out for three to four days, 24 hour per day, until the shallow waters beyond were covered with countless numbers of brightly colored buoys, each marking the location of a fisherman's traps.

With tens of thousands of crab pots destined to be set by the fleet as a whole, it was vital for the fishermen to get their gear set out on the fishing grounds where they had plenty of room to set the gear without tangling other fishermen. The longer a fisherman took to set his gear, the harder it would become to find a suitable place to set safely inside the shipping lanes used by the big ships that constantly transit in and out of the Columbia River on their way to Portland, Oregon to drop off and pick up their cargos. In this regard, I was fortunate to be running one of the larger boats in the fleet, capable of carrying over 300 of the circular crab traps, each weighing 80 pounds and covered with stainless steel wire mesh.

The Ballad

The Ballad is a solid boat, making up for what she lacked in creature comforts, with a seaworthiness that exceeded her relatively small size. "She may be cantankerous," I'd said many times referring to the uncomfortable ride in heavy seas, "but she'll always bring you home." At sixty-six feet long and nearly twenty feet wide, the *Ballad* build a whaleback design, meaning that her cabin is located at the bow of the boat, and the wheelhouse is situated above that on an upper deck that extends towards the stern nearly a third of her length. When outfitted for crab, she carries no outriggers or booms, with only a single mast towering forty feet above her main deck that holds four great big sodium lights capable of lighting up the sea for nearly an eighth of a mile, and two mercury vapor lights that shine down on the deck. She carries a full compliment of high-powered radios and navigational equipment, and her twin 350-horsepower diesels are capable of pushing her through the water, fully loaded, at 11 knots in calm weather. She was known for her rough ride, but I had fished her in extreme weather and believed her to be, pound for pound, one of the toughest boats in the fleet.

Playing a Hunch

Bouncing my way across the bone-jarring, mud-filled potholes, I pulled into the parking lot of Pacific Coast Seafoods where Jeff and Steve were busy re-rigging the mountain of crab pots that took up a substantial part of the parking lot. The potential earnings in the Dungeness fishery begun to attract boats from other fisheries that were declining in profitability, and although a limited entry system had been put into place, the numbers of pots in the water increased dramatically as the competition grew fiercer. During this time, I noticed a trend in the fishery that I attributed to this increase in effort. The shallow waters near shore where we traditionally enjoyed our best fishing simply weren't producing large catches of crabs as consistently as they had in the past.

My theory for this change was simple: I believed the sheer numbers of pots in the deeper waters offshore created a formidable gauntlet that the crabs must pass through on their way to the shallow inshore waters, and the large volumes of crabs we fished in previous years simply weren't getting through. During the time we were on strike, I reasoned that a large number of crabs might have a chance to make their way into the shallows. Deciding to gamble that my theory was right, I instructed my crew to re-rig the majority of pots we were planning to fish, changing the longer lines that were added to fish the deeper waters back to the shorter ones that would be used for the inshore waters. The 300 pots aboard the Ballad were already rigged with short lines, but I wanted another 300 ready for our second load. With some reluctance, they threw themselves into the considerable task and had been working day and night in the cold rain and mud to get the job done before the gun went off.

"People buy into the leader before they buy into the leader's vision."

~John C. Maxwell~

"How's it going guys?" I asked as I got out of my truck.

"Hey, Smitty. We've just about got 'er done. Maybe twenty more pots or so." Steve replied. He fished aboard the *Ballad* for two years and was a firecracker. Young and strong, he reminded me of myself in the early days in my own fishing career. An oversized kid, he was a fast learner, immensely strong and at 20-years old was determined to be running his own boat before he turned 25. The hardships that are a part of a fisherman's work out at sea didn't seem to bother him much, and I remembered watching him as we were hauling gear in a storm the previous year.

I been surprised to look back and see him swinging a pot aboard, wearing nothing but his rain pants and a hooded sweatshirt. Icy cold waves were crashing across the deck on a regular basis, and he was thoroughly soaked. I asked him over the loudhailer if he wanted to stop to put on some dry clothes and a raincoat. With wet hair plastered across his forehead, he simply shook his head, waved his hands forward, and yelled, "Let's go!" He was as game as they come, and I admired him for his enthusiasm.

Jeff walked up to Steve and me, as we stood talking in the drizzling overcast. His bright orange raingear took on the same brownish color of the parking lot from working in the rain. "Hey, what's going on with the price? Are we gonna go fishing soon or what?" he asked, a cigarette dangling from his mouth. He was our "fill in" man, and although this was his first season working for me, he was an experienced hand and no stranger to the Dungeness fishery.

The last several years, I needed to hire an additional crewmember each winter. I required three crewmen aboard for the Dungeness fishery, and of the four who regularly fished with me during the summer longline season in Alaska, one held a berth on one of David's (the boat owner) other boats fishing the Bering Sea, while the other had his own Dungeness boat to run. I worked with both men for years, and they were among some of the best crewmembers I had ever known. So, while I was bit aggravated having to hire a new man each year, I was willing to put up with it in order to have them on board during the summer.

"Looks like we'll know tomorrow," I answered. "Good job on the gear, Guys. Where's Marty?"

"He's over at the gear shed getting the rest of the buoys loaded on the trailer," Steve replied.

"Yeah, okay. Soon as you're done, you can take off, but make sure you're on the boat by 8:00 in the morning. We have a meeting scheduled for 8:30, and I want the boat warmed up and ready to go in case they reach an agreement on price." I didn't need to worry about whether they would show up or not. In my ten years as a Captain, the vast majority of my crewmembers were hardworking men who took their jobs seriously. Ever since the million-pound Dungeness season the second year David owned her, the *Ballad* gained a reputation as a moneymaker, and under both David's and my command, crew turnover was relatively low.

"A business is a reflection of the leader. A fish doesn't stink just from the tail, and a company doesn't succeed or fail from the bottom."

~Gary Feldmar~

A Few Good Men

Jobs aboard Highliner boats are hard to come by, and most crewmembers were simply not willing to risk loosing their berths. I had a low tolerance for crewmembers that did not show up or did show up but were too hung over to work. When they first signed aboard, I would tell them that frankly, I didn't really care what they did while ashore, but I expected them to be at the boat and able to work when asked. They would get a warning the first and second time; then they would be down the road.

Most of the long-term crewmembers that worked for me were seasoned veterans, and, I included, had been down the road of hard drinking and bar crawling, extremely prevalent in the fishing industry. That road lead to nowhere, and we all squandered away hundreds of thousand of dollars getting nothing in return but hangovers and a bag full of stories that would be of no interest to anyone but another party animal. I suppose I was lucky, but missing crewmen and debilitating hangovers were something that I only had to deal with a few times as a Captain, and true to my word, down the road they went.

Fighting onboard was another issue that rarely came up, and I have always believed fighting onboard to be a result of either lack of effective leadership or having the wrong mix of people onboard. Spending months at sea in what amounts to 300 square feet of living space is stressful enough, but putting four or five naturally aggressive men into that space, tempers can flare in a hurry. Therefore, one of the things I looked for when hiring a new man was a good temperament and an ability to get along with others. In my view, building a mediocre crewman into a hotshot in a relatively short amount of time was always easier than trying to get someone who was already a hotshot *and knew* it to change his attitude. Problems? Down the road.

I hopped back into my truck and drove and bounced my way back across the potholes on my way to the gear shed, Steppen Wolf's *Born to Be Wild* blaring from the stereo at earsplitting volume while I sang along at the top of my lungs, "Get your motor runnin'; Head out on the highway; Looking for adventure; Whatever comes my way…" I was cranked up for the season, and the wait was driving me nuts.

"Enthusiasm is the electric current that keeps the engine of life going at top speed. Enthusiasm is the very propeller of progress."

~B.C. Forbes~

Pulling into the parking lot of the gear shed, I turned off my truck, got out and walked through the big bay door where Marty greeted me. He was attempting to throw a bundle of buoys up onto the top of an enormous pile of fishing gear that was growing perilously high on the back of the 40-foot flatbed trailer hitched to his Ford F-250 pick-up truck. "Hey, Smitty! How's it going? Mmrrrffff!" he called out as the bundle of rock hard polypropylene buoys cascaded back down off the pile onto his head. At 35-years old, Marty worked aboard the *Ballad* for the last three years and was one of the most likeable men I ever sailed with.

If I looked up 'positive personality' in the dictionary, I would have found Marty's picture peering back at me. In the three years that he worked as a crewmember aboard the *Ballad*, I never once heard him complain. Instead, everything always seemed to be an adventure, and he was given to surprising us all with the unexpected.

I looked over at Marty as he finished tying the awkward orange bundle to the top of the trailer. "What's happening?" I asked, "Is that the last of the buoys?"

"Yup," he replied. "This is it. We put all of the extra line from the pots in the parking lot into the back fish hold. The bait freezer's full, and I've got eight totes of fresh, hanging bait on standby in the refrigeration room at the cannery. What's the outlook on price?"

"Well, I talked to Whitey a little while ago, and we'll probably be able to go tomorrow morning. We have a meeting at 8:30 in the morning, so we'll know then for sure," I replied. "Why don't you take off and go home for the night."

"Sounds good, Boss. I'll be down by 7:30 and check everything out so we'll be ready to go if the strike ends," he said. Marty was the *Ballad's* engineer and the kind of guy that I didn't even need to suggest warming the boat up. When the meeting was over, the engines would be running and the electronics turned on. All I would have to do was step aboard, have the guys cast off the lines and steam down the river for the ocean beyond. And the next day, that's exactly what happened.

CHAPTER THREE
Opening Day

"People who take risks are the people you'll lose against."

-John Sculley-

"What a day!" I thought grinning from ear to ear as the Ballad leapt forward, the throttles to their limits, "What a day!" The season was barely two days old, and the boat was already half full. We hadn't even put all of our gear in the water yet!

As I maneuvered the Ballad into position to retrieve yet another crab pot, I remembered getting a call on the cellular phone as we were steaming back up the river at full speed after setting our first load of gear. David called to see how things were going. He was one of the finest fishermen I ever met, the best Captain I ever worked for as a crewman, and as a boat owner, he was eager to assist in any way he could.

"How's it going, Smitty?" he asked.

"Pretty good. We're just passing buoy number nine on our way up the river. We caught the tide just right… coming in on the flood. We should arrive in about an hour. What's the dock look like? If we can get to the dock right away, we should be able to do a turn-and-burn and catch the ebb tide back out," I replied.

"Looks good right now. A couple of boats are at the dock right now, but they just about have their loads on and should be out of here by the time you arrive. I'll get some guys to start bringing the gear for your next load out onto the dock so it'll be ready for you as soon as you get here. Where'd you put your first load?"

"Well, I put one long one, 150 pots from the river up to Willipa Bay in 15 fathoms. Then I set two 80 pot strings, one in 14 and the other in 13 fathoms up by the Willipa," I answered.

"You what?! What'd you put them there for? We've never caught any crab up there before! Why didn't you put them in the usual spot?" he asked, clearly upset at what he thought was a tactical mistake. During the past eight years, we always started the season fishing the same grounds before moving, catching what crabs we could before moving to "greener pastures." This plan worked well, too.

The Early Days

I started working as a crewmember aboard the *Ballad* in early 1987 with her owner David Lethin at the helm. At over six-feet with a shock of brown hair and intense brown eyes, he is one of the hardest working men I have ever met. He has an unnatural ability to get people to see things his way, and nearly everything he touches turns to gold. During the years I worked for him, he taught me volumes about the fishing industry, and he always proved to be fair although somewhat demanding at times. He never held an air of superiority over his crews, a trait that can be found on many boats, and is well liked and respected by those who work for him. The fact that at 40-years old he was a "Highliner's Highliner" and has proven time and again to be flat out one of the best fishermen working the West Coast and Alaska doesn't hurt either. In only 12 years, he built a fleet of boats that includes the *Ballad*, a salmon gill-netter, and two Bering Sea crabbers that he owns in partnership with Don Jester who also owns our partner boat, the *Sea Valley II,* and one of the few men I know that is David's equal as a fisherman. All of them are top producers.

The *Ballad* was one of the most successful boats out of a fleet of hundreds that participated in the Dungeness crab fishery off the coasts of Washington, Oregon, and Northern California. So why hadn't I followed our usual routine and set the gear the same as in years past? Call it a hunch, but something compelled me to break ranks, and I decided that the shallows off the northern coast of Long Beach would be where we would find crabs.

I held the phone tightly as David waited for an answer to his question. "Well, uh, I think we'll find crab up there. Besides, we never really fished much in that area," I answered, sticking to my guns but still compromising a bit. "I'll run in and check a few after we dump this next load. If we don't catch anything, we'll move 'em. We only put 160 pots in there, and we're way ahead of everybody else at this point." By his reply, he did not sound convinced.

A Hunch Pays Off

Now, just a day later, my hunch was about to pay off. I set our second load of gear in two long strings, 10 miles long, each in deeper water than the previous strings, before running inshore to spot check the pots that came into question the previous day. With a low swell running out of the west and a slight chop caused by a light northwest wind, the water was blue with reflection from a sky that was accented by heavy clouds here and there that promised a turn for the worse weather-wise in the coming days. I looked back to ensure that my crew was ready to start hauling. They were wearing the usual uniform for a day such as this: brown knee-high rubber boots, sweat pants, and hooded sweatshirts, and they were all covered from chest to ankles in bright orange, heavyweight rain pants. The whole ensemble was completed by various colors of baseball caps, the bills of which were stained by the dirt, grease, grime and fish slime from constant adjustments during past fishing trips with hands protected by long, orange rubber gloves.

"You guys ready?" I asked.

A chorus of hoots and hollers was accentuated by a loud banging as Marty slapped the side of the boat with the "V-shaped" stainless steel hook protruding out of the end of a twelve-foot bamboo pole he held ready in his hands. As the block man, he would use the "hook-pole" to retrieve the buoys from the water, throwing them onto the deck as he slapped the buoy line into the crab block hanging next to him, just outside the bulwarks. The block was capable of winching the 80-pound pots nestled on the sandy bottom a hundred feet below in less than twenty seconds, and getting a hand caught in the block at that speed would earn a man a helicopter evacuation to the hospital. I learned that lesson during my first King crab season when a friend of mine had his arm torn off the first day of the opener. Since then, I knew too many fishermen who been injured or lost, and I collected my own numerous sets of x-rays, stitches and scars.

"Speed is the result of efficiency"

~Steven R. Smith~

As was my custom, I pulled up to the first buoy and said a prayer for the safety of my crew. No matter how the season played out, my first priority has always been to bring my crew home safely. Although I gained a reputation as a "driver", for fishing tough weather, and pushing my crews hard, I never had a man seriously injured, and I wanted to keep it that way. Luckily on this day, the weather was fine, my crew was working well together, and they all knew what was expected of them.

So, with the hoots and hollers of a crew excited to pull the first crab pots of the season drifting off with the wind, I maneuvered the boat into position. With a quick movement, Marty deftly sent the hook-pole out, retrieved the buoys, and soon had the crab block reeling the pot up from the sand eighty-five feet below.

Picking up the microphone for the loudspeaker on deck, I gave the usual command, "Start out stacking." I wanted to make sure we started stowing the pots on board so we could move them to the same fishing grounds where we started the season so many times in years past, should my hunch prove wrong.

I heard a cheer as the pot broke the surface of the water. Looking back, I could scarcely believe my eyes. Dangling from the crab block was the fullest pot of Dungeness crab I ever saw! It was literally stuffed full to the point that no more crabs could have crawled in if they wanted to!

"Set it back, right?" the crew asked in unison as they pulled the pot aboard.

"Are those all keepers?" I asked in disbelief, as I ran out on the upper deck to watch them dump the crab out of the pot. The only Dungeness crab pots I ever saw that were even remotely close to being as full as the one we just brought aboard that was full of undersized juvenile crabs.

"Yeah, they're jumbos! You want to set back?" they asked again, the excitement filling the air.

"No, we'll stack one more, and if it's even half as full as that one is, we'll start setting back then," I replied, my heart beginning to pound with anticipation. I then ran back into the wheelhouse and throttled up the *Ballad's* big twin engines to race up to the next pot as Jeff carried the now empty steel cage 40 feet to the stern and set it on the ironwood deck.

The next pot was again greeted with cheers as it was swung aboard. It was an identical twin to the first pot, stuffed full of crabs with their legs waving as they poked out through the stainless steel mesh.

"Stack that one, too, and we'll start running this string and setting 'em back. That way, we'll have a couple to set if we find a gap in the string," I instructed the guys, who by this time were a flurry of arms and elbows as they counted and measured the dump-box full of massive, tan colored crabs that were doing their best to pinch anything and everything in sight. "I suppose it's a good thing that we have another eighty-pot string less than an eighth of a mile inshore huh?" More cheers, and off we went to start hauling and setting back the 78 pots that lay in front of us, their bright orange buoys disappearing in the distance, stretching out by the northerly current in a neat, perfectly straight row that resembled the lights on an airport runway. And set back we did. We roared through the string of gear in less than two hours, stopping only so that the crew could catch up measuring the abundance of crabs coming aboard.

Luck seemed to be with us. The tide changed right as we finished and was now flowing from the south, parallel to the wide, sandy beach dotted with scrub bushes and drift logs. Our next string lay just inside the line of breakers visible three miles inshore, a relatively short distance by marine standards. Instead of running all the way back to the southern end of the string just inshore of the one we just pulled, our run time to the next string had been reduced from half an hour to just five minutes.

More cheers rose as the first pot swung aboard, just as full as the pots in the previous string. Obviously, we had set on a heavy concentration of crab. "Yahoo!" I hollered over the loudspeaker. "Let's rock and roll!" and away we went, repeating the same drill we finished just minutes earlier. Another two hours, and we were finished. In just four hours, we put almost 12,000 pounds of crab aboard. This was by far and above the best Dungeness crab fishing I had ever heard about, let alone experienced.

"OK guys. We're gonna head back and spot-check some of the pots in that first string we pulled. Then, we'll head back to the river and get another load of gear." Setting the autopilot on course for the southern end of our first string, I was just settling myself into the Captain's chair when I heard a shout from the back deck. Instinctively, I reached for the throttles as I turned my head towards the deck just in time to see Marty begin parading around the back deck with a giant octopus on his head that he retrieved from the last crab trap hauled from the water. No hat, no hood…nothing but forty pounds of octopus cascading down to his shoulders. The crew was laughing and pointing as he danced around the deck in a sailor's jig. The octopus was not amused at all and soon got its revenge by holding fast to Marty's neck with its tentacles when he tried to take it off. Several minutes of comical struggling and pleading for assistance from the rest of the crew went by before Marty eventually managed to get the poor animal off and throw it back into the sea. "What am I gonna tell my wife?" he hollered in astonishment when we all roared with laughter at the sight of the quarter-sized red hickeys the octopus' tentacles left all over his face and neck. Yes, what a day this was indeed!

Overflowing With Abundance

As we pulled up to the very first pot we hauled just four hours earlier, I called back to the deck where the crew was eagerly waiting at the rail, ready to go to work, "They've only been soaking four hours so they probably won't have much in 'em, but if it is better than a 15 average in 'em, we'll haul 'em again."

"Roger that!" came the reply as I swung the boat around and pulled up along side the buoys. I waited with anticipation as excess buoy line peeled from the block with a loud, throaty ripping sound that permeated the afternoon as the pot was hauled through the water. Marty stood at the rail peering intently into the water, his left hand on the hydraulic valve controlling the block. Stop it too late and the pot could slam into the block, tearing the wire mesh or worse, break free from the water with its momentum turning it into a potentially dangerous, 80-pound steel missile sailing through the air across the deck. Stopping or slowing it too soon would result in valuable seconds being lost. At first thought, those few seconds lost wouldn't seem like much, but given the sheer numbers of crab pots a typical Dungeness crab boat hauls each day, lost seconds can quickly add up to hours of lost production time in the ultra-competitive fishery.

On this fine day, I was blessed with a block man who was not only bringing the buoys aboard with lightning speed but was also very skilled at bringing the pot up quickly and smoothly. I looked back to the deck as I heard the block come to a stop, followed by yet another loud cheer. Hanging from the block, the pot we hauled just hours earlier looked the same as when we hauled it the first time! "Right on!" I hollered over the loudspeaker, "We're on 'em big time! Let's run 'em again!" And with that, I pushed the throttle to their limits to run to the next pot.

Suddenly the phone rang. David was on the line. "Have you had a chance to check those pots up by the Willipa yet?" he asked.

"Yeah," I replied in my best monotone, in an attempt to hold him in suspense. "We've checked a few."

"Anybody home?"

"Yeah, a few." But, I couldn't contain myself any longer. "As a matter of fact, they're absolutely stuffed! We got about 120 pounds per pot in both strings, so I ran back to check the first one we hauled, and it looked the same as it did the first time! We're almost done running the first string for the second time, then we're gonna run the other one again and head for the dock. It's unbelievable, Dave! We might get a full load out of just these two strings with no other boats are around!"

"Great!" he answered, "Good call! Maybe you can catch all the bugs up there then move down to our regular spot and scoop 'em up there, too. I'll let the cannery know you'll be at the dock with a load in around 10 hours and get your next load of pots out on the dock and ready to put aboard as soon as you're finished unloading."

"Sounds good. I gotta take care of business here, so I'll see you when we get back!" I hung up the phone and spun the boat towards the string that lay just inshore as Marty pushed the last pot in the string overboard and into the water to begin its long fall to the ocean floor below that I now knew was teeming with crab.

Staking a Claim

Having offloaded 24,000 pounds of crab, 24 hours later we were steaming back out across the bar with another full load of pots. We unloaded our catch is less than six hours. We were still on schedule to reach our goal of being the first boat to have all of its gear in the water, but the weather was beginning to kick up a bit. I welcomed the increasing winds. The worsening weather and increasing swells that it brought with it would force many of the fishermen to wait to the incoming tide before transiting their boats, heavy in the water with the tons of steel pots on their decks in or out across the bar at the mouth of the river. The immeasurable power of the incoming flood tide when it collided with the water pouring from the mouth of the river would actually stop the flow and cause the river to change direction and flow upstream for several miles. With the water flowing in the same direction as the ocean waves, the swells on the bar would be smooth and rounded, allowing safe passage for the fishing boats making the crossing.

When the tide changed to the ebb and the waters once again started flowing out of the river, their collision with the larger incoming ocean swells caused by the worsening weather would make the bar an inhospitable and dangerous place of towering waves capable of smashing out windows and spinning a boat sideways, where it could then be rolled over by the crashing waters. To lose a boat on the bar during a strong ebb tide would mean certain death for the men onboard. A rollover is perhaps the most dangerous situation that any mariner will face. Trapped inside the cabin by the inrushing waters as the boat begins to sink, a quick death by drowning is almost assured. The unlucky few who make it out of the confines of a boat rolled over on the bar face the longer struggle against hypothermia caused by the frigid waters as they are swept far out to sea. The powerful river current as it combines with the outbound tide causes a plume of silty-green water that can stretch five miles or more out to sea. To find a man enduring such a fate would be next to impossible before he succumbed to the cold waters, which is probably what happened to the crew aboard the Andrea Gail, most notably portrayed in the movie *The Perfect Storm*.

Heading out across the bar during the period of calm as the tide changed from flood to ebb, the *Ballad* was carrying its last load of pots. We wouldn't need to wait the 12 hours before the tidal cycle was completed. Instead, we would set the pots onboard in the same area we hauled previously and then begin fishing in earnest.

"Somehow I can't believe that there are any heights that can't be scaled by a man who knows the secret of making dreams come true. This special secret, it seems to me, can be summarized in four C's. They are curiosity, confidence, courage and constancy, and the greatest of these is confidence. When you believe in a thing, believe in it all the way, implicitly and unquestionably."

- Walt Disney -

When we reached the fishing grounds that had been so productive for us the previous day, I was happily surprised to see that almost no other boats had set their gear in the area. That patch of ocean was ours to set our gear as we wished. We immediately set out four more strings alongside those already in the water and began hauling and setting back pot after pot, bursting full of crab. As we fished, the wind continued to increase until it seemed to level off at a steady 25 knots, bringing with it heavy, gray storm clouds releasing torrents of rain. While making for a rough ride, the weather was still within the realm of being more of an inconvenience to the task at hand than a handicap. The reports I was receiving from the National Weather Service broadcast indicated that it would soon subside. My crew would have become nearly indistinguishable from each other if not for the various scribbles and pictures they drew all over the heavy, hooded raincoats they donned to protect themselves from the heavy rains and sheets of sea spray as the *Ballad* was pounded by the sharp, ten-foot seas being pushed by the wind.

We stacked and moved the majority of pots from our second load that we set in the deep until we had close to 700 pots fishing in the shallow waters. I now knew beyond any doubt that every pot held a very heavy concentration of crab. Every pot that we pulled yielded an immense catch and now, after nearly 18 hours of work without a break, our fish hold was overflowing with abundance. Checking my watch, I smiled with the realization that we would reach the river mouth just as the tide changed from ebb to flood, allowing for a safe bar crossing and a quick run up the river to the cannery. We would unload our crab, restock our supply of bait and groceries before returning once again to the rich fishing grounds of Willipa Bay.

As I once again turned the boat to the south and set course for home, I settled into my chair for the three-hour run to the river. Yes, this was a fine day indeed!

CHAPTER FOUR
Perseverance

"You can measure opportunity with the same yardstick that measures the risk involved. They go together."

~Earl Nightingale~

"C'mon guys, lets get while the getting's good!" I hollered out the back door as Marty and Steve yanked open the lid of the pot, quickly flipping it upside down and back again, dumping another 50 crabs into the already full dump box. Steve pushed the freshly baited pot over the side, its buoy line trailing behind the boat, and I was greeted by a series of whoops and holler's as I pulled up to the next pot. Steve turned back to the dump box where Jeff was still sorting crabs while Marty reached out with the hook pole. Seconds later the block was screaming out again as another pot started its quick trip to the surface. He also turned back to the dump box, and soon all three were all arms and elbows as they frantically tried to sort as many crab as possible before the pot in the block hit the surface. They were hauling over 100 pots per hour, light speed as far as the Dungeness fishery was concerned, and the volume of crab was beginning to overwhelm them.

Two pots later, Marty called up that the dump box was full, and they needed some time to get caught up. Pulling the boat out of gear, I walked out on the deck overlooking them and cheered them on. I hated stopping. Anytime a pot wasn't in the block, we weren't catching crabs as far as I was concerned. I constantly pushed my crews to work faster and faster. The guys were in overdrive, and I wasn't sure how they could go any faster, but I cheered them on anyway. I paced nervously back and forth, every once in a while looking ahead to make sure we didn't lose our position with the next buoy that was waiting just off the bow.

> *"There are countless ways of attaining greatness, but any road*
> *to reaching one's maximum potential must be built on a bedrock*
> *of respect for the individual. A commitment to excellence*
> *and a rejection of mediocrity."*
>
> *~ Buck Rogers ~*

"Alright, you guys are smoking!" I shouted as they approached the halfway mark in the pile of crabs in the dump box, "Nobody can touch you guys!" I was answered by another cheer from the arms and elbows. They knew they were flying through the gear and loved every minute of it. The fact that the last week produced some of the best Dungeness fishing any of us had ever seen didn't hurt either. We had a good head start on the rest of the fleet in the race to be "Number One," and we wanted to keep it that way.

I couldn't stand it any longer and ran back for the wheelhouse and shoved the throttles full ahead. "Let's roll! Whoever hauls the most gear wins! You guys want it?" Another cheer and seconds later another pot was in the block. Waiting for the pot to break the surface, I thought back to an earlier season aboard the Ballad, to another banner season of pushing the envelope with the pedal to the metal.

Getting the Jump on the Competition

Mid-July during the summer of 1992 found the Trinity Islands Dungeness crab fleet anchored securely in Lazy Bay to wait out a summer storm. With storm warnings posted for the Kodiak area of the Gulf of Alaska, the open sea was surely a dangerous place of unrivaled ferocity. Unusual both for the time of year and its intensity, the wind was gusting to nearly 100 knots. The dark green tundra, covering flanks of the mountain towering over the Wards Cove processing plant, were utterly barren. The mammoth, gleaming white "Hollywood" sign placed there by cannery workers that welcomed mariners to Lazy Bay was gone, having blown away by the unrelenting winds that screamed across the bay.

Throughout the previous night and into the day, gusts of wind known as "williwaws" that resembled mini-tornadoes and hit with a similar ferocity danced across the water, colliding with the boats resting at anchor and heeling them over as the powerful winds raked through their masts and rigging with a howling intensity. I was beginning to re-think my decision to anchor in Rodman's Reach.

"Rodman's," as we called it, is a small sliver of water less that an eighth of a mile wide that snakes its way southward through the middle of the peninsula that marks the entrance to Alitak Bay at the far south end of Kodiak Island and the open sea beyond. A cozy and popular anchorage, it is lined on one side by rocky bluffs covered with tundra and patches of brush, with relatively flat grasslands on the other. Marked by numerous tiny inlets to land a skiff, we called the bluffs on the east side "The Deer Farm" due to the abundant herds of deer that inhabited its rolling terrain. The interior held several small ponds with beaver dams, and the far western edge, where the hills ran down to meet Alitak Bay, made for excellent clam digging. Less than three hours from the crab grounds, "Rodman's" was a favorite of the Dungeness fleet during "off-days." While letting the gear soak, we enjoyed exploring its secrets many times in the past.

I considered running all the way to the head of Alitak Bay to wait out the storm in Alpine Cove. Protected from the weather on all sides by peaks towering straight up from the water to heights of 4,500 feet or more, the wind rarely blew there, regardless of what kind of weather was slamming into the island. The mountains were a brilliant emerald green during the summer months with the tallest peaks holding onto their caps of snow. Numerous small streams wound down through the narrow valleys between the mountains then fanned out across a small delta marked by high grasses before spilling across the tidal flats and into the cove.

All in all, Alaska is a sportsman's paradise. The mountains offered outstanding hunting, while the cold waters below were teeming with salmon that came home to spawn. During our visits, we would often spend the day zipping around the cove in our inflatable skiff looking for schools of salmon, catching and releasing until our arms ached. Dinners were fresh salmon, deer steaks or King Crab retrieved from a pot set in the middle of the bay. It was a wonderful place to relax and play, but mostly, we came for the bears.

The Alaska Wilderness

Kodiak brown bears are considered some of the largest in the world and can reach sizes of 1,500 pounds or more. I once counted 18 bears in the grassy delta at the head of Alpine cove as they gathered to fish for the salmon struggling up the creek. Lane and I often would spend hours sitting in the grass with a pair of binoculars, watching them go about their business, which could be a bit nerve-wracking when walking in the bush. The brush was so thick that often the only way to get around was by using the many game trails that traversed the area. More then once we came around a corner and ran head on into what seemed at the moment to be a giant mountain of deadly brown fur as the bear reared up on its hind legs to get a better look at us. But often as not, the bear would be more afraid of us than we were of him (if that was possible) and would turn and run, crashing through the brush, leaving us laughing as we tried to keep our feet on still shaking, very rubbery legs.

I sat in my chair thinking about past adventures in Alpine Cove, and the lure of a restful night's sleep in a quiet harbor without needing a man on watch at all times to insure we didn't drag anchor was strong. But my competitive attitude and desire to be top boat insisted that we remain "on the pick," remaining in Rodman's Reach until after the storm.

The storm was forecast to diminish in the afternoon, and the winds were finally beginning to ease a bit. We had been on anchor for two days waiting the storm out, and I was anxious to get back out fishing. Picking up the tide book, I began studying the predictions for the area. To reach the fishing grounds located on the south sides of where Sitkinak and Tugidak Islands lay, we would need to pass out of Lazy Bay, across the wide expanse that marked the entrance of Alitak Bay, and through the treacherous Tugidak Passage. "The Pass," as we called it, was a narrow, shallow waterway that made its way between the short gap between Sitkinak and Tugidak Islands. Winding its way between ever-shifting sandbars, The Pass was marked "*Foul*" on marine charts, a warning to mariners to stay away. With no buoys, fathom marks, or other navigational indicators, Tugidak Passage was considered passable only with 'local knowledge' and extreme care during an appropriate tide.

Normally, we would time our departure so that we could catch a free ride out through the pass on an outgoing tide that could flow as swiftly as a river. My experience with the Columbia River bar, though, taught me well the dangerous conditions that could arise when an outgoing tide rushes headlong into storm waves. Due to the present weather, that option was out of the question. Instead, I decided to make the transit just before the incoming tide reached the high-water mark. Just like a river bar, I knew that the deeper water at high tide and the incoming flow of water would help to diminish the swells rolling up into the channel. The only unnerving part of my plan was the timing. We would need to make our crossing in the cold, darkness of midnight. If, that is, the weather came down as forecast.

Suddenly, a loud "Pop!" reverberated through the boat as another gust of wind slammed into the *Ballad*, heeling her over, causing the heavy anchor cable leading down to the murky depths below to pull tight and jump across to the other side of the narrow bow roller. Not uncommon when anchored in heavy winds, the sound was un-nerving nonetheless. As the williwaw passed, I glanced up at the sheer cliff rising straight up from the water, less than 100 yards in front of us. A pair of bald eagles built a nest on a small ledge about two-thirds of the way up its face that they called home for several years. They didn't seem to be struggling quite so hard to hold onto their perch on the rock face, and a quick glance out into Lazy Bay confirmed that the winds were indeed diminishing as forecasted.

Competitive Edge

Making my way down to the galley where Lane and Big D were deeply immersed in a high-stakes game of cribbage, I told them of my plan and asked for their input. I was sure we could make it work, and while ultimately the decision would be mine and mine alone, they fished with me for several years, and I valued their opinion. The basic idea was that if we could sneak across at midnight, we could have a 12-hour head start on the rest of the fleet in the good-natured competition that flourished among some of the boats on the fishing grounds. A hard-driving crew, they were always game to "go for it," and they all agreed it was at least worth going out to take a look.

Excited about the prospect of blazing the trail through the stormy waters, I set our departure time for 10:00 a.m. Then I went back upstairs for another look at the tide book, set the watch alarm for 9:30 a.m. and sat back in my chair to continue reading the novel I was working on during the last couple of days.

Just as Zog the Terrible was about to demolish the planet Terron with his battle cruiser, the watch alarm announced that departure time had come. Closing my book, I glanced out the window towards the bay, then walked over and tapped on the barometer. It was still rising, and the winds came down nicely, maybe blowing around 25 knots or so. I quickly fired up the *Ballad's* big twin diesels, woke up my crew, and we were soon underway. As we rounded the corner of Lazy Bay, I reached over and set the autopilot on a course that would take us southward along the western coast of Alitak Bay and across the open waters beyond to the Trinity Islands. Noting that the winds were holding steady, I picked up the tide book to study it again.

During my years as a skipper, I fished extreme weather in the open ocean many times, but transiting potentially hazardous waters inshore always made me nervous. My eyes would dart quickly back and forth as I constantly scanned my navigational equipment, looking out the window then to the depth sounder, radar, GPS, and plotter. Every couple of minutes, I would make the three steps to the chart table and check for hidden dangers I might have missed the first hundred times I looked at it, before returning to the helm to start the process all over again. In some areas, I wouldn't even bother with the chart. These areas were either uncharted or simply shaded blue and marked "Foul" just like Tugidak Pass. No matter how many times I had been through a particular pass or across a reef, I seemed to grow new gray hairs with each crossing. But the mountainous swells that we were sure to meet in the Pass added a whole new dimension to the picture.

Two hours later found us running along at full throttle against the incoming tide that was flooding between the two islands. Making just over seven knots, the Ballad rounded the corner between Tugidak and Sitkinak Islands, holding just over an eighth of a mile off the sand spit as we made the sharp right turn to follow the narrow channel, running roughly parallel to the beach for the next two miles. Up ahead, we would cross two shallow, rocky reefs where we would have less than 10 feet of water under the keel, followed by a 90-degree left turn and then a three-mile transit along a narrow channel between treacherous sandbars out to the open sea beyond. With a direct southeastern exposure, the swells would be running straight up the channel.

Here I would find out if my gamble would pay off. If my calculations were wrong, the results could be tragic. A dangerous attempt to turn around in immense, breaking seas on an inky black night while staying off the sandbars would be dicey at best.

My hand tightened on the helm as I looked at the display on the video depth sounder mounted in the wheelhouse. It turned from the pleasant, speckled green and yellow that indicated a soft, sandy bottom to the angry red of solid rock as it started its relentless march upward. We were approaching the shallow water over the reef.

I had been through Tugidak Passage countless times before, and I knew the secrets of navigation through its narrow confines. I saw its many moods, yet this one particular stretch still gave me pause. Pushed by a four knot current, we would pass over the reef with just ten feet of water between the keel of the boat and the solid rock bottom.

Flashback

As I watched the depth sounder display peak at just over 1.2 fathoms before beginning its descent, indicating the relative safety of deeper water, I chuckled as my mind wandered back to my first journey through the pass, back to those earlier days of great anticipation and high expectation, unfettered with the possibility of failure.

"What's the secret to catching Dungeness crab anyway," I asked David, "Should I look for depressions in the sea floor or set the pots on banks and on top of ridges? When's the best time to fish? What about tides? Storms? Bait?" I peppered him with questions, most of which I already knew the answers to but nevertheless looked for assurance that my answers were right while at the same time wishing he wasn't there so I could get on with my new job as Captain.

"Watch what kind of bottom you're fishing in. As a fisherman, you can live and die by this machine right here," he said tapping the depth sounder, his eyes twinkling at my eagerness. "Other than that, just find a patch of sand, and put a pot down there. Wait awhile, then pull it up and see if anything's in it. If there is, put it back. If not, find another patch and do the same thing."

Now, several years later, I had 1,200 crab pots sitting on 1,200 patches of sand, a ready boat and a willing crew. I was taking a gamble and taking the principle of effective, consistent action to the extreme. My competitive side knew well that in any aspect of life, all things being equal, that "whoever hauls the most gear" wins. And this was a game I wanted to win very badly, but I didn't want to make any stupid mistakes in the process.

Whoever Hauls the Most Gear Wins

As we made the 90-degree left turn in front of the Tugidak Lagoon, I stared intently out the windows as if through sheer force of will I might see any breakers directly in the channel in front of us. Off to the edges, the seething maelstrom of whitewater caused by what were obviously huge waves crashing onto the sandbars glowed pale orange in the reflection of the large sodium lights on the mast. Ahead, I could only see blackness.

I backed off on the throttle a bit as we continued out of the channel. The swells were beginning to increase in size substantially as the deeper channel waters near the island yielded to yet another shallower portion farther out. I looked at my watch: 12:20 a.m. With a high tide forecast for 12:27, our timing was perfect.

As we slowly ventured out, I kept a sharp eye on the condition of the swells rolling through the pass. The depth sounder was rendered almost useless, showing depth ranges of 15 to 50 feet as we crested each of the 20-foot swells, followed by the plunge to the trough that followed. I eyed the Loran closely to make sure we remained in the channel and away from the dangers of the nearby sandbars.

The ride wasn't particularly a rough one as the swells, while immense, were also smooth, with well rounded crests, evidence that my theory that the incoming tide would knock the waves down was correct. Still, I was nervous as we continued out the channel, my crew silent as they stood in the wheelhouse beside me.

Soon the swells subsided in size, but the crests started to sharpen as we began to reach deeper waters where there was less tidal influence. My gamble appeared to be paying off! Another 30 minutes, and we were free of the channel and out on the crab grounds. The wind was still blowing from the southeast at 20 knots, and the seas were sharp, causing the boat to begin to buck hard as we made our way to our first string of crab pots. But all in all, the weather seemed to be diminishing rapidly and the weather, while uncomfortable, was quite fishable.

And fish we did, pulling up pot after pot, full of gleaming bright Dungeness crab! We worked throughout the night and when the dawn arrived, we were greeted with a pleasant surprise. The sky cleared, and the morning sun shone brightly upon the now, relatively calm waters in explosions of brilliant golden sparkles.

Now that the storm was over, I knew the fleet would be returning to the fishing grounds soon, but our gamble the previous night gave us a 12-hour head start hauling gear. I could hear the other skippers talking on the radio, having awakened to diminishing winds, they began the transit across Alta Bay towards Tugidak Pass and out to the crab grounds beyond. Before long, I received a call.

"Hey, Steve, are you on this one?" came Marko's voice on the VHF radio.

"You bet Marko. What's up?"

"Hey, when we got up this morning, we noticed you guys had left. Are you out fishing or did you move to another bay?" he asked.

"We're fishing," I replied with a grin, anticipating the next question.

"Good on ya! What's the weather like out there? It's still kind of squally in here," he asked.

"It's beautiful, Marko. We've got a light, southeast breeze, no seas, and a low groundswell out of the southeast," I replied, as I looked back to see yet another pot full of crab come aboard.

"Sounds good," Marko replied, "We're on our way!"

Two hours later, I listened to the talk on the radio as several boats attempted to come through the pass, only to meet steep breakers, with one of them nearly losing a stack of crab pots on the back deck. Due to the unsafe conditions in the pass, they turned around and were proceeding to safe anchorage on the other side of Tugidak Island.

"Hey, Steve," came Marko's voice, "Where's this great weather you were talking about? I don't see any blue sky, and the pass is a mess."

Checking my watch and looking toward the pass, I started to chuckle. A fog bank settled over the northwest end of Tugidak Island, and the outgoing tide was running hard against the southeasterly groundswell rolling up the channel. "I duuno," I replied. "The weather is beautiful out here. We came through last night on the flood tide and didn't have any problems at all."

"Yeah, I see," came Marko's response. "Well, we'll anchor up here and wait for the tide to change, then try it again."

I hoped that none of the other skippers thought I gave them a faulty weather report. Of all the fisheries I participated in, the Dungeness fishery off the Trinity Islands was the one I enjoyed the most. All of the fishermen got along well and looked out for each other. And I wanted to keep it that way. I liked and respected all of them, and most had far more experience at this game than I did. I called Marko back to assure him that when they did get through the pass, they would find fine fishing weather.

Six hours later, we were greeted on the crab grounds by the sudden appearance of the boats that waited out the tide on the other side of the island. The summer crab fishery was soon back to its usual form with lots of friendly banter over the radio as they hauled aboard the bounty of crab that awaited them in their pots that crisscrossed the shallows of the Trinity Islands in gleaming rows of brightly painted buoys. Our gamble paid off. By late evening, we filled the boat and were steaming back to town to unload our catch, make a quick turnaround and get back on the grounds.

Pile "Em High!

"Smitty! The box is full. Can you stop so we can sort crab again?" Marty's shout yanked me out of my reminiscence, away from Alaska and back to the grey-green waters off of Long Beach with a jolt. I looked back at the arms and elbows flying about the dump box, sorted crab flying this way and that, then back out the window in front of me.

"Nah, we've only got three more pots in this string. Put 'em in the bait box if you have to," I replied. "You can get caught up on the way to the next string. How's the hold looking?"

"We're almost there," came the reply. The fish hold was full to the point where the hatch in the dump box was stuffed full of crab, and they took to filling garbage cans with crab, dumping them into the main hatch in an effort to take advantage of every spare inch of hold space available. "Maybe 30 more pots, and she'll be full."

Two hours later, the hold was stuffed to the top. We were only two hours from the mouth of the river; however, with four hours to go until the ebb tide slacked off, we had time to kill. I hated stopping, and I was not going to just bob around doing nothing when I knew our pots were full of crab. Besides, the weather forecast indicated that the unusually calm weather we had been enjoying would be coming to an end in the next several days, and I wanted to put as many pounds in as possible before the weather became an issue.

"Great things are not done by impulse,
but by a series of small things brought together."

~Vincent Van Gogh~

"Hey, Boss, what's up?" Marty asked, as he re-appeared at the wheelhouse door behind me as I stood pondering my options in the golden glows of the sun as it slipped below the horizon.

"We're gonna have to wait a few hours for the tide to change," I replied. "I don't wanna sit here, though. Can you guys rig up some kind of barricade on the deck in front of the fish hold?"

Understanding what I was after, Marty grinned at my question. "You got it, Boss!" he answered as he turned around and ran back down onto the deck, hollering as he went. "We're gonna go for a deck load!"

Normally, the fish hold of a crabber is filled with constantly circulating seawater to keep them alive for delivery to the processor. I knew that Dungeness crab were hardy creatures, and I figured that if we could get them unloaded within the next six hours or so, they would be fine. I grinned as I turned the boat towards the beach and set course for our farthest inside string. I brought in deck loads before, filling the 5'x5'x4' plastic totes we used to carry fresh bait in, but I had never done anything like what I now had in mind.

"You guys ready?" I asked over the loudhailer as I pulled up to the first pot in the string. A chorus of shouts and banging sounds indicated the affirmative, and soon the guys were back to arms and elbows, more motivated than ever as I pushed the boat ahead harder than ever in a non-stop cadence of throttles and turns that was punctuated by howling diesels and a screaming crab block.

"That's it guys, we gotta head for the barn," I announced, as the last pot in the string was pushed over the side. In place of the usual cheer in response, I got a series of protests as the crew urged me to haul more gear. I chuckled to myself as I set course for the river. "Those guys have the fever, and they have it bad," I thought to myself. Instead of the usual mix of exhilaration at a full load and relief that they could finally get some rest after two days without sleep that I expected, they became so caught up in putting crab aboard they wanted to keep going! To have a crew like this was a fishing boat Captain's dream, but as I surveyed the giant pile of crab that nearly filled the front half of the deck, I wasn't sure we could put any more aboard anyway. Besides, I wanted to catch the tide up the river, get unloaded as quickly as possible and get back on the grounds before the weather turned ugly. Turning back to the business at hand, I made a slight adjustment to the autopilot, pushed the throttles nearly to their limit and sat back in my chair to start counting the miles to the river.

CHAPTER FIVE
The Red Line

"You don't have just one chance to win,
but you don't have unlimited opportunities either."

~A.L. Williams~

"He did good, didn't he?" David asked as he elbowed Whitey in the side, the characteristic twinkle in his eyes a dead giveaway that he was enjoying every minute of the proceedings as we stood on the Pacific Coast Seafood's dock looking down at the immense pile of crab covering the front half of the *Ballad's* main deck.

Whitey, on the other hand, was not happy at all. We were not the only boat enjoying good fishing, and the abundance of crab being caught and delivered quickly overwhelmed the cannery's ability to process them. They were forced to limit the number of pounds that each boat would be allowed to bring in. In an attempt to give everyone a fair shake, they limited the larger boats to 28,000 pounds per delivery and the smaller boats to 12,000 pounds.

Looking down at the pile of crab below, Whitey groaned again. "Yeah, he did really well, but that's not the point! What am I going to do with that mess? We're backed up nearly 18 hours already, and I've got guys in the parking lot looking for extra totes. Even then, I don't even know if we've got enough totes to get all of that off! How much do you think you've got on, Smitty?"

"I dunno," I shrugged, "Maybe 50,000 pounds." I was trying hard to contain myself and couldn't help cracking a smile as I answered.

"He did good, didn't he?" David laughed as he elbowed Whitey again.

"David, knock it off!" Whitey answered, "This is ridiculous!" This wasn't the first time a scene like this had been played out between David and Whitey. They were a regular occurrence when David had been skipper of the *Ballad*. He had an uncanny ability to get people to see things his way. I remembered a season in the late eighties when Whitey gave up in frustration, throwing up his hands, and said, "Whatever, David, just go fishing." And go fishing we did, bringing in load after load until we delivered over 800,000 pounds in just over four months. The season before, we topped 1,000,000 pounds, and to this day, it is the biggest season I have ever heard of in that fishery. I knew that in this case, as in others, they would work things out. I know David enjoyed it, and perhaps in some ways, Whitey did as well. He was a good man and looked out for all the fishermen who delivered to Pacific Coast. He was willing to go the extra mile for them, especially the top producers like the *Ballad*.

"Hey, Steve," I heard at my shoulder followed by "Whoa! What a load!" "You guys got the pedal to the metal all the way to red-line!" I turned to look at Marko as he and the rest of the unloading crew stepped up onto the timber at the edge of the dock, looking down with mouths open as they pulled on their gloves. "Yeah, nice trip! That's what we liked to see!" The canneries on the West Coast didn't provide unloaders as the processors in Alaska did. They left it up to the boats to either unload their own catch or hire out to Marko's crew for the job. Fast and efficient, most boats paid by the pound for their services to unload their catch. Big loads meant quick money.

Jumping down to the deck, Marko waded into the pile of writhing crab and started tossing them by the handful into the bucket hanging from the dock crane. With fingers covered in athletic tape and heavy gloves over them, he worked quickly to keep the aggressive crabs, still very much alive, from clamping onto his fingers. I stood and watched the first few buckets as they were winched up to the dock while David still discussed the merits of my transgression with Whitey. Then, turning my back and marching into the cannery, I went in search of 7,000 pounds of bait. I wasn't going to worry about trip limits; I just wanted to go fishing.

CHAPTER SIX
Humility

"Awareness of both your limitations and your potential enhances humility."

~Sheila Murray Bethel~

Wicked Waves

"…Guys! Big wave coming! Get under shelter and hang on. And I mean hang on!" I hollered over the intercom. With no place to hide and nothing to do but wait for the impact of hundreds of tons of icy, crushing water that was sure to follow, memories of past fishing trips flashed through my mind as the *Ballad* rested almost peacefully, bow facing the open sea that we crossed so many times in years past. My ego got the best of me, and my decision to try to retrieve the gear in an area that moments before was unthinkable was just plain stupid. I felt untouchable during the past week and a half since we had been enjoying some of the hottest crab fishing I ever experienced. And now everything might come to an end under the terrible, crushing weight of hundreds of tons of icy, deadly water.

I leaned forward in my chair, staring up at the huge mountain of water towering up over the Ballad. My heart stopped cold as the top of the enormous wave became a translucent green, the sun shining through the water as it reared up ever higher until the top disappeared from view as it rose up over the wheelhouse windows.

With a shudder, the boat stopped cold as if it ran into a brick wall. I ducked down behind the dash and a loud "POP" echoing like a rifle shot through the wheelhouse as tons of green water rolled over the bow and slammed into the windows in front of me, blocking out the sunlight and plunging the wheelhouse into darkness. Thank God the windows held, preventing the tons of icy water from flooding the cabin! Then just as suddenly, I was airborne. The 80 plus tons of aluminum that made up the *Ballad* fell away beneath me as the boat broke through the backside of the wave. Time seemed to stand still for an instant when the boat continued its dark, downward plunge before ending in a shuddering "BOOM" as she landed hard on the water behind the wave. Grabbing the loudhailer microphone as I crashed back down onto my chair with a jolt, I spun around to see a foaming mountain of water begin to subside over the back deck. My crew was nowhere in sight.

"Are you guys OK?" I shouted into the microphone.

"Yeah, we're here…" came the reply followed by an assortment of hoots and hollers. Luckily, they managed to run for the shelter offered where the upper deck hung over the main deck near the entrance to the galley.

The back deck was completely submerged, and the tops of the rails that surrounded it were just beginning to break the surface of the water as the *Ballad* struggled to break herself free from the tons of icy water that buried her. The 100 crab pots that had just moments before been a perfectly square stack stretching from rail to rail was now a jumbled pile of tangled lines, buoys and pots hanging from the rubber strands of their lid hooks. The water that surrounded the boat was a riot of flotsam as lines, buoys, bait jars and hook poles floated off the deck. The crew was rushing about madly trying to retrieve what they could, pulling lines in, heaving pots back aboard and throwing gear in a pile in the center of the deck. But the sea wasn't finished with us yet.

Looking forward, I saw another wave that wasn't as huge at the first but still big enough to roll us over if we were caught broadside. I needed to use the engines to power the boat around to face the wave head-on, but looking back at the tangle of lines that surrounded us, the thought of the big propellers sucking the line down and wrapping themselves in a huge, twisted mass of polypropylene that would stall both engines was a real concern. Still, I had no choice. I saw this area covered by huge breakers as we hauled the first part of the string, and apparently, the momentarily calm water that lured us in was a fluke. We barely survived the immense wave without any structural damage and another was bearing down on us. We had to somehow get to the safety of deeper water.

My first thought was to push both engines to full speed ahead, but if the floating line fouled the propellers, we would be at the mercy of the waves, and the result would almost surely be a disaster. Chances were none of us would survive the icy cold waters and huge breakers that pounded the beach. We were in a very dangerous place, and I couldn't expect any boats to put themselves in a similar situation by coming to our aid even if anyone was close by, which they weren't.

Less than 30 seconds elapsed since the impact of that first wave. I gingerly put one engine in gear, feeling the vibrations of the big propeller as it turned for the telltale sign that it was becoming entangled, and watched the line floating in the water at the stern. The *Ballad* was blessed with having two propellers, and if one became entangled, I would have one more chance with the other.

The water that covered the back deck was slowly receding, pouring through the scuppers at the base of the rails. The boat was still very heavy and slow to respond, but ever so slowly she came about to face outwards towards the oncoming sea with no time to spare.

"Here comes another one!" I barked over the loudspeaker as the crew, having seen the second wave approaching, scrambled for cover. Once again I heard a loud "Crack!" as the wall of water collided with the wheelhouse windows followed by a tremendous shudder as the boat landed in the trough behind the wave. While the wave was not nearly as violent as the first, given the confusion and mess that the back deck had been left in, the effect was the same. Once again the crew was waist deep in chilling seawater as they attempted to keep as much gear as they could from floating away.

Again and again, the maelstrom created by towering, breaking waves pounded the Ballad as she clawed her way towards deeper water. My crew braved the onslaught as they continued to grab confused armloads of gear from the water and throw them towards the center of the deck only to repeat the process as the boat collided with another wave. Keeping one eye on my crew and one on the approaching waves, I struggled to keep the boat on course, daring only to engage one engine at a time in an attempt to keep the propellers clear.

Finally after one of the longest 15 minutes of my life, we managed to break free of the breakers and into the deeper waters beyond. The back deck was a complete mess. Piles of crab pots lay strewn across the deck with the lines and buoys that were normally stored inside them heaped in a huge tangled jumble. Behind us I could see a trail of buoys and bait jars that were swept overboard floating in the water. The rest of the gear the crew used to repair broken pots, as well as the extra bait that was set out to thaw, simply disappeared. An inspection of the outside of the wheelhouse revealed no more than a broken antennae and a loose strap holding the life raft in place. With nobody hurt and minimal damage resulting from our ordeal, we were very lucky.

"It is no great thing to be humble when you are brought low;
but to be humble when you are praised is a great and rare attainment."

~Saint Bernard~

With quite a bit of line still trailing in the water behind the boat, I still had only the port engine in gear while the boat's autopilot took us on a course straight offshore. As I stood in the wheelhouse door surveying the mess below me, the radio suddenly crackled to life. "Wow! That woulda' made a heck of a picture but not one you'd want to show your insurance company, Steve!"

Turning back to face the open ocean that lay before us, I picked up the radio microphone to reply to whoever just called. "Yeah, who just called here? Please repeat?" I asked, my knees still shaking.

"Yeah, Steve, it's Berl here on the *Chandallar*. We're just outside of you about a mile or so. I was just saying that it would have made a heck of an exciting picture the way you guys came off those waves, but I don't think your insurance company would have seen it that way. You guys OK?"

"Hi, Berl. We're fine. Got a big mess to clean up on deck, but no real damage. I'll tell you what though…that was scary. I have never been through anything like that in my life. We were hauling gear, and I saw those big waves in that one spot…must've been caused by a rip tide or something. Anyway,

I figured we'd just write off the pots we had in but when we got up there, the water just laid down flat, so we went in. Next thing I know, we're getting hammered," I answered, sitting down in my chair to stop my knees from shaking. "I wasn't sure we were gonna make it out of there in one piece."

"I can imagine," Berl radioed back. "We're running a string here in about 15 fathoms, and I was just admiring the huge breakers inshore. I had no idea you guys were even in there until I saw your boat come blasting out of the middle of one of those waves. You guys looked like a Coast Guard surf rescue boat practicing on the Columbia River bar."

"Hey, Steve, ya still got this one on?" came another voice from the radio.

"Yeah, I get you fine, Dennis, how's it going?" I answered.

"Oh, we're just going through the motions out here." Dennis Sturgell, the Captain of the *Bold Contender*, joined in. "Hey, I was listening to you and Berl talking. Glad you made it out of there. For what it's worth, I just wanted to let you know they build crab pots every day, my friend."

Lesson Learned

Dennis was one of the most successful fishermen in the West Coast Dungeness crab fishery. He fished these waters for over twenty years as a Highliner and probably forgot more about Dungeness crabbing than I learned in my five years as Captain of the *Ballad*. We competed hard for the top spot that season and much of our radio conversations were good-natured ribbing with stories intended to keep the other off balance, but his last comment was on the level and was words of wisdom from a friend. "They build crab pots everyday" was simply a reminder that in the high-stakes game we were playing out on the crab grounds, we could gamble with strategy and gear placement but never with the safety of the boat or its crew.

During my years as a Captain, I gained a reputation as one who would fish extreme weather but with safety as my first priority. I never rolled the dice the way I did one hour earlier. The success I enjoyed in the ultra-competitive Dungeness crab fishery, especially in the last two years, went to my head, and it nearly cost me my boat and the lives of the men who were depending on me to make decisions that would keep them safe.

After we cleaned up the mess on deck and re-stacked our crab pots, I set course for a string well offshore, leaving the pots that remained in the shallows to be lost to the enormous waves. In the breakers off Long Beach, the sea offered me a strong lesson in humility that I would never forget, but unbeknownst to me, a series of fierce winter storms was on its way, and class was just getting started.

CHAPTER SEVEN
Perseverance II

*"Most people give up just when they're about to achieve success.
They give up at the last minute of the game,
one foot from a winning touchdown."*

~H. Ross Perot~

Turning up the VHF radio mounted on the white, acoustical tile ceiling of the wheelhouse as if by making it louder I could somehow change the National Weather Service forecast I just heard, I listened intently while keeping a sharp lookout for breakers as we crossed the mountainous swells that were rolling across the Columbia River bar during the flood tide.

The fishing was beginning to slow down somewhat but during the first few weeks of the season, we enjoyed some of the best fishing I ever saw. With close to 275,000 pounds in for the season, I was tempted to stay in town for a few days of well-earned rest. The weather took a turn for the worse during the last several days, and my main concern at this point was the tending of our gear. I was still somewhat shaken up by our experience in the breakers off Long Beach the second week of the season, but we continued to fish the productive grounds in the shallows. We had several hundred pots set along the 14-fathom curve and while they should be too deep to be affected by the storm waves, I wanted to make sure before the seas had a chance to scatter them up and down the coast.

While a small number of fishermen often seemed to use poor weather as an excuse to sit in the coffee shops and grouse about their poor fortune, most of the men in the fishery were hard working, seasoned veterans who would put out to sea when the weather and river bar conditions permitted to begin the endless process of setting and hauling their traps. Because of gale-force winds now lashing the coast and the huge swells that they brought with them, fishing wasn't even an option at this point for many boats in the fleet due to their smaller size, and their Captains wisely returned to port. The Ballad was a tough boat, and pound for pound one of the most seaworthy I ever fished on. Besides, the *Sea Valley II, Bold Contender* and *Pacific Prospector* were still out fishing. The friendly competition among the four boats was fierce, and we would often fish to the limits of our boat's abilities to handle the weather in our quest to be "Number One." To my knowledge, we would be one of only four boats that chose to continue fishing in the storm tossed waters.

The voice blaring forth from the radio continued its dry, emotionless roll call until it once again broadcast the weather forecast for our area. "From Cape Shaowater to Clatsop Spit and out 60 miles: West winds 30 knots increasing to 35 knots by mid afternoon. Westerly swells to 28 feet. Rain. Outlook: West winds 40 knots."

"Great," I muttered as I throttled back to slow the boat's approach to a particularly large wave. "Ain't that a peach?"

> *"You got to know when to hold 'em. Know when to fold 'em.*
> *Know when to walk away. Know when to run."*
>
> *-Kenny Rogers (The Gambler)-*

The weather was deteriorating towards the end of our last trip. With gale warnings forecast to push an 18-foot swell into the coastal waters, we stacked all of the gear we used fishing in the shallows out to the deeper waters outside of the 14-fathom curve we called the "safe zone." When the swells kicked up to 15 or 20 feet, as they often did when frequent storms battered the rain soaked coasts of the Northwest, the surge of the huge waves on the lines and buoys that marked the rows of crab pots set in the shallows could mean trouble. As the seas started to build, each wave that passed over the gear would pull hard on the buoys as they struggled to stay afloat. This constant tugging on the pot sitting on the soft sand below would soon cause it to sink. As the wave heights increased, soon the entire sea floor would become a swirling mass of water, the crabs burrowing into the sand for protection. The seas would push vast amounts of sand across the bottom. Worse yet, the surge of water along the ocean bottom could turn the circular pots up on their sides where they would begin to roll, sometimes being swept for a distance of ten miles or more.

Scattered Gear

After the storm passed, a fisherman unlucky enough to have left any gear in the shallows would be forced to spend days looking for pots. A lucky few might wash up on the beach and be found then thrown into the back of a fisherman's pickup truck, hopefully to be given back to its owner. The rest were found by guesswork. By determining the likely direction of drift and searching the hundreds of square miles of ocean along the beach, they would be found in scattered clumps, sometimes with ten or more buoys tangled together in tight clusters of brightly painted buoys.

For the majority of pots that did not wash up on the beach, those that a fisherman did find were often buried up to 20 feet in the sand, killing the crabs trapped inside and making retrieval of just the crab pot all but impossible. This scattering of gear was a yearly occurrence, requiring fishermen to keep a sharp eye on the weather and moving their pots out of the shallows into the deeper waters of the "safe-zone", then back into the shallows as the storms came and went. This repeated stacking and setting of gear was grueling work, but it was part and parcel with the fishery and a necessity if a fisherman wanted to reap the harvest brought on by the immense schools of crab that frequented the shallows in search of feed.

Although most of the boats in the fleet carried special pumps used to retrieve the pots from their dark, cold graves, the work required very calm weather, a rare commodity at this time of year. Besides, it was very time consuming and backbreaking work. On a good day, instead of hauling and setting back 400-800 pots, a boat might only retrieve 20 "stuck" pots, and all of the crabs they contained would be dead. The bottom line was that if a fisherman had any amount of gear in the shallows when a storm came ashore, the results could be disastrous to his gear inventory (very costly) and /or his fish production during a limited season.

On the *Ballad*, after three long and very uncomfortable hours of pounding through the mountainous waves, we arrived at the location of our gear. As the swells passed by, I could see the bright orange flashes of the row of small buoys marking our first and shallowest string of crab pots bobbing back to the surface with each wave that passed. Our set hadn't moved a bit and was right where we placed it. As we began hauling the string of pots, the crab block would stop momentarily before resuming its typical roar as it pulled the pots from the sand below, the slight pause indicating that the swells caused the pots to sink slightly into the soft bottom. Although the pots were lightly stuck, the amount was acceptable. We set them just at the edge of the "safe zone," and my cautious approach appeared to have paid off. Set any shallower at all, and they would all have become hopelessly stuck.

Rivalries

Although the wind was increasing and the swells were immense, we were able to continue running our gear, albeit at a far slower pace than I would have liked. Still, I wasn't too concerned by our progress. The Captains of the three other vessels and I gained somewhat of a reputation for fishing severe weather, so we tended to carry a somewhat perverse sort of pride, constantly joked with each other on the radio that if we all agreed to head back to port and wait out the weather, we would. Nobody ever wanted to be the first to cry "Uncle," though. Besides, even if we could run only 200 of our pots per day, that was still 200 pots worth of production that we were gaining in the hard-driving competition to be among the top producing boats in the fleet with the rest of the fleet in port.

In all of the fishing ports along the coasts of Washington and Oregon, a bitter rivalry existed between many of the fishermen who ran the smaller boats in the fleet and those who captained the larger vessels that were far less constrained by poor weather. Ever competitive, many of those who owned the smaller boats resented the bigger, more seaworthy boat's greater carrying capacity and ability to keep fishing when the weather turned foul. The owners and captains of the larger vessels, nonetheless, saw it differently. If the fishermen who manned the smaller boats wanted to compete with them, they reasoned, they should then take the same financial risks they had and go out and buy a bigger boat. Economics aside, a good case could be made for either side depending on one's point of view. The situation remains, and the rivalry continues to this day, causing a sad division among the fishermen, the majority of whom, albeit aggressive, hard working men, seek to only make a living upon the sea.

"Winners make goals; Losers make excuses."

-Anonymous-

An unfortunate result of this rivalry was a thinly disguised attempt by a group of fishermen in Washington to ban the larger vessels based in Oregon from fishing the lucrative crab grounds off the Washington coast, which they had done so for years. In spite of this, the plan backfired when Washington legislature passed a law many of the Oregon-based boats appealed in court and were given permits to fish their traditional grounds.

Oregon and California soon followed suit and established limited-entry systems for their own waters as well. A result of this privatization of the fishery is an increase in the numbers of pots fished by the smaller boats. In addition, the new rules attracted the attention of larger boats based in distant ports that purchased permits from fishermen leaving the fishery. Far from reducing the pressure on the crab stocks, the first year alone saw a 100% increase in the number of pots being fished, and the grounds became more crowded than ever.

Mountains and Valleys

But as the storm waters raged along the Washington coast, a new weather forecast focused my attention ever more on the immediate task at hand. Political conflicts were the furthest thing from my mind.

During the last 12 hours, the wind surpassed the 35 knots that had originally been forecast and was now blowing close to 45 knots, pushing huge swells that topped 33 feet in from the deep ocean waters offshore. We were close to the limits of severe weather that we could withstand and keep fishing.

The boat slid down the waves into the troughs between them that resembled deep valleys bordered by towering, dark green mountains of water topped with snowy white crests of foam when the tops of the waves collapsed upon them. If the weather worsened any more, we would be forced to point the boat directly into the weather and begin idling just fast enough to maintain steerage as we clawed our way offshore.

Returning to port was no longer an option because the giant swells rolled across the bar at the mouth of the Columbia River, slamming head on into the flood engorged waters that poured forth. With a straight coastline that was devoid of any bays in which to seek shelter or islands to hide behind, the entrance to the only safe harbor available was now a maelstrom of treacherous currents and deadly breakers in excess of 40 feet. In addition, the Coast Guard closed the bar to navigation by vessels of any size, including the giant container ships bound for Portland, 60 miles up river.

Success is a Matter of Attitude

Inside the wheelhouse, my white knuckled hands ached as I held on to the throttle levers and rudder control, bracing myself as the boat rolled hard with each passing wave. Literally sitting on the edge of my chair, my feet were pressed hard against the cabinet to my left that held the TV-like navigation plotter in an effort to brace myself against the wall and keep from being thrown across the carpeted floor and into the opposite wall 15 feet away. Out on the deck, my crew was having an even tougher time of it. The westerly swells were forcing us to haul our gear broadside to the weather, so they were exposed to the full fury of the storm as wave after wave slammed into the side of the boat, battering them mercilessly with sheets of frigid water.

My head felt as though it were on a swivel as I looked forward to keep the next buoy in sight, then to my right at the oncoming waves, then forward again. Every so often a wave bore down on us that was bigger and steeper than its brothers, and I was forced to push the throttles to their limits in an effort to power the boat around and punch through the wall of water head on, using the bulk of the boat to protect my crew from the power of the onrushing water. The *Ballad* rolled hard to starboard as another wave passed beneath us, blocking my view of the oncoming seas. As the boat righted itself, I looked up to see a foaming crest of whitewater bearing down on us. Allowing no time to shout a warning over the loudspeaker on the deck, the full force of the wave crashed over the rail, my crew disappearing as they were swept from their feet and washed across the deck into the rail on the port side.

Turning the boat head on into the seas, I looked back as they picked themselves up and ran over to their places at the rail. They were tough men and willing to keep working, but they deserved a break. Picking up the loudhailer microphone I decided to let them make the call. "You guys want to take a break or keep hauling?" I asked.

Like most fishermen, they were driven by the same, strong sense of competition that compelled the four boats currently weathering the storm to leave port. None of them willing to be the first one to give in, my question was greeted by silence as they stood in their positions, their eyes peering up at the wheelhouse from under the thoroughly soaked baseball caps that poked through the small, circular openings provided by the tightly tied hoods of their raingear. I knew well enough from my own experiences as a crewman that an answer of silence to such a question meant, "Keep hauling!"

"You guys are hard core!" I said, rewarding their perseverance. Such compliments go a long way on the deck of a fishing boat, and by letting them make the decision to keep working or not, I demonstrated my respect and appreciation for their hard work. "Why don't you come in and get something to eat and put on some dry clothes. I don't think anyone else is fishing anyway."

As they disappeared from view to remove their gear, I turned up the VHF to listen to the weather forecast that promptly promised more of the same with no end in sight. The intensity of the storm seemed to have leveled off, but our catch was terrible, averaging just over eight crabs per pot instead of the 20-40 average we should have enjoyed during the first few days of the season. From what I was hearing from the other three boats on the grounds, everyone was experiencing the same thing. With the heavy weather making any kind of move to new fishing grounds impossible, the trip was off to a dismal start. I set the boat on course for a slow jog back inshore that would give my crew a needed and well-deserved rest. And before we started running through the gear a second time, I stared angrily at the waves, as if through sheer force of will I could calm the storm.

CHAPTER EIGHT
The North Coast

"Most bold change is the result of a hundred thousand tiny changes that culminate in a bold product or procedure or structure."

~ Tom Peters~

Towards the end of December, the fishing off Long Beach slowed considerably, but a brief lull in the storm track allowed the weather to finally begin to subside over the last week. The heavy gray clouds and torrents of rain gave way to brilliant blue skies, a light wind out of the southeast and a swell that finally diminished to less than 15 feet, but the devastation that visited upon the gear set by the fleet during that last week had been complete. The duration and intensity of the heavy swells wreaked havoc on strings of crab pots in waters as deep as 35 fathoms and ten miles offshore. Of the thousands of pots that fishermen set in the shallows, those that remained were scattered across 50 square miles of ocean hopelessly buried deep in the sand. The rest simply disappeared entirely.

My decision to keep running our gear was both a blessing and a curse. While our constant hauling and setting of our pots in the deep helped to keep them in a semblance of order, my decision to run the gear in the "safe zone" was a major mistake. Instead of getting stuck and remaining where we set them as they most likely would have if I left them alone, the pots we hauled were drug off to join the confusion of tangled lines and buoys littering the inshore waters. The catch we delivered from that trip was less than 20,000 pounds. I took solace in that it was the biggest catch of the four boats that went fishing that week, a small consolation for the costly gear we lost.

"The rewards for those who persevere
far exceed the pain that must precede the victory."

- Ted Engstrom -

After days of searching for lost pots, we gathered our gear into some impression of order and continued fishing. We did not have our "pot pump" on board, and I didn't see the need to go back to town to get it given that relatively few of our pots became stuck. For that, I was grateful. I remembered many times aboard the *Ballad* as a crewmember when we would spend days pumping out 100 pots or more only to have another storm roll inshore and get them all stuck again. The name of the game in those days was to fish as many pots as close to the breaker line as possible and with the constant winter storms, we were always taking a gamble. But this season, we had been lucky. Our pots did not get stuck but rather scattered to the north, swept along by the enormous waves. We were able to retrieve many of them without having to pump. The few that were stuck were not going anywhere, so I marked their position on the plotter and planned to pump them out at the end of the season if I couldn't talk someone else into doing it for me. I had other plans: I was taking a season off.

I had been through the drill many times before, and the decline in production off Long Beach told me the time had come to move to new grounds. Taking advantage of the fair weather, I decided to move up to the fishing grounds around Destruction Island some 120 miles to the north. The grounds to the north were fished by the big boats out of Westport, Washington, but given the limited number of them, the grounds were not fished out nearly as quickly as those off Long Beach, and we were usually able to find good fishing there late into the season. Of all the boats in the fleet that were capable of making the move, only four of us made it consistently. I never quite understood why more boats did not move but was glad that they didn't. Instead, many of them seemed content to battle it out with countless other boats for a rapidly dwindling supply of crab.

Searching For New Grounds

We had nearly 150 pots onboard, stacked in neat rows, each layer overlapping the one below it with the pots on the ends braced against the rails. While the work wasn't nearly as grueling as manhandling the 700-pound pots and 50-pound coils of line used in the Bering Sea King and Opilio crab fisheries, the quicker pace made it backbreaking work nonetheless. As each pot was brought aboard, the lines and buoys were coiled inside, and a crewmember would pick up the pot to carry it to the ever-growing stack, set it in place and run back for the next one. Then again, my crewmembers were used to it given my penchant for stacking the majority of the gear that we hauled. I was constantly moving our gear around as I tried to stay with the schools of crab roving the sea bottom in search of feed. Today was just like any other day for the crew with the exception that when we had a boatload of pots. They would be rewarded with a 12-hour nap as we steamed for Destruction Island.

By noon we had 300 pots on board, and I set course for the island while Marty and Jeff stuffed the plastic bait jars with chopped squid. Steve was bent over one of the bait totes making hanging bait "rigs" by running stainless steel hooks through the fish carcasses we brought out from the cannery. As each pot was set, it would have one bait jar and a hanging bait rig from its center. After the pots settled on the sea floor, the crabs would follow the scent of the bait up the current and crawl through one of the two entrance tunnels placed on opposite sides of the pot in an effort to find a meal. At the inside end of each tunnel, two metal bars hung down that were built to only swing inward so that after the crabs passed through them they would be trapped inside. Because crabs give off a chemical "scent" when they are feeding, the hanging bait gives them something to eat, thereby, attracting even more crabs. Not terribly scientific, but it works. As soon as the guys finished with the bait, they came inside, and we all enjoyed our first hot meal and good night's rest since the season begun. When the fishing slowed down and we weren't stacking gear, the crew rotated in and off the deck for four hours apiece. I would stay at the helm for days on end, every so often catching a quick catnap while one of the crew drove to the next string. During the trip to and from the cannery, the crew had an opportunity to sleep, while the four hours or so that it took to unload the boat was mine. The stormy weather left us exhausted, though, and the beef rib dinner quickly disappeared. The boat was reduced to silence save for the low thrum of the engines as each man retired to his bunk for the deathlike sleep of a mid-season fisherman. Marty volunteered for the first watch. I wrote down directions for each of them to stand two-hour watches, stay fifteen miles offshore, and check the engine room and the circulation pump on a regular basis.

While the big circulation pumps of a crabber are necessary to keep the crabs alive, it can be deadly for the crew if they fail. Drawing fresh seawater from the sea chest valve located near the keel in the engine room, the pump pushes enough water through pipes in the bottom of the fish-hold to completely replace the water every 20 minutes or so with the excess draining out of the hatches at deck level. Should the pumps should fail, the water will begin to drain back through the circulation pipes and out of the fish hold. As the water level drops and it begins to slosh around, the weight of the moving water soon puts the boat's ability to right herself after a roll into jeopardy. With a full load of pots onboard, the Ballad would reach the point of no return quickly, and she would roll over.

As my head hit the pillow on my bunk in the wheelhouse, I took one last look at Marty, who was already on the cell phone to his wife, and my eyelids slammed shut.

Destruction Island Waters

Almost instantaneously, I heard someone calling me from far off in the distance. "Hey, Smitty!" the voice was calling up from the back deck. Busy as I was, I held up my hand for silence. My hand was firm on the helm as I attempted to steer the big trawler through the rush-hour traffic that clogged the freeway ahead of me. Several hundred yards behind me, I could see the giant net I was towing dragging along on the pavement. Without warning, a big Cadillac Fleetwood suddenly changed lanes and drove right over the top of the net. I leaned out the wheelhouse door and gave the driver the finger as he zoomed by. I had a hard enough time trying to catch fish on this stretch of Interstate 90 without having to deal with crazy drivers. "Hey, Smitty!" I heard the voice call out again. A terrible shudder went through the boat, and everything started to turn gray.

"Hey, Smitty! Wake up!" As my eyes fluttered open, I looked up at Steve who was shaking me by the shoulders. "Hey man, wake up. We're at the waypoint where you wanted to get up."

"Yeah, OK," I mumbled as the unreasonable dream of freeway fishing faded. I rolled out of bed and looked out the window. "Good," I thought to myself, "the weather's still holding." After checking our position, I slumped into my chair and stared out the window at the flat, gray, featureless sea ahead. I picked up the steaming hot cup of coffee Steve brought up and took another sip. I began to feel a bit more alive as the caffeine coursed through my veins. Four hours to go. The radar showed two contacts close in near the beach. Picking up the binoculars, I scanned the coastline in an effort to see who they were, but the light mist that started to fall made it impossible. Setting the binoculars back down, I walked back to the chart table, examining marks and indicating both depth and bottom composition. I had done it a hundred times before and already decided where I wanted to set, but it was a way to pass the time.

I always enjoyed fishing the second half of the season off the north coast of Washington State. As we traveled north, the low hills and flat beaches gave way to rugged cliffs and sea-stacks backed by the magnificence of the Olympic Mountains. The far northwestern corner of the Olympic Peninsula is largely uninhabited, and the coast where the mountains meet the sea is accessible only by boat, giving it more of a wilderness feeling than the crowded fishing grounds to the south where the lights of the coastal towns often glitter in the night.

"Goals give you the specific direction to make your dreams come true."

~Bob Conklin~

With the autopilot set to maintain a course parallel to the beach, I watched the depth sounder intensely as the colors changed from an angry red-orange that indicated a rocky bottom to the yellow-green hues that indicated sand. "Trail it!" I called over the loudhailer, and I throttled the boat up to 1100 rpm's, my preferred setting speed, as Marty threw the first buoy over. As the buoy drifted away behind the boat, Marty threw the coil of line over the side while Jeff pinned the bait inside the next pot. When the line came tight, Marty pushed the pot over the side and reached for the next one as Steve dropped it on the rail beside him. Pot after pot, they set over the side with the row of orange buoys marking the pots growing behind us as we went.

Three hours later, we set out six, 50-pot strings and were steaming south back towards Long Beach for our next load of gear. The next 30 hours would bring another 12 hours rest followed by six hours of stacking gear, followed by yet another 12 hours of travel time. By the time we had two loads of gear up by the Island, we would be caught up on sleep, refreshed and ready to rock and roll. The rest would be welcome, but with another big low-pressure system tracking its way across the North Pacific, we were running out of time.

CHAPTER NINE
Deliverance

"… give us this day, our daily bread and deliver us from evil…"

~ The Lord's Prayer ~

Two months later, the season was essentially over. Only a few crabs were left to catch, and our production declined drastically. We steadily moved our gear northward from Destruction Island along the coast in an attempt to find new grounds that had not been fished. Having set gear nearly to Cape Flattery that marked the desolate northwest corner of Washington State and finding nothing worth fishing, we recently picked up a full load of crab pots and were moving them back down below "The Island" for one final shot at finding crab.

Tough Call

As we ran south past the jagged, gray cliffs marking the edge of where the seemingly endless forests of the Pacific Northwest met the sea under the shadows of the Olympic Mountains, once again the weather begun to take a turn for the worse as it did so many times in the proceeding weeks. Gale force winds were forecast for the area, and as the winds increased, they pushed ever-larger seas towards the shore where they crashed with ferocity upon the rocks. We were bone tired from fishing nearly non-stop for two months. Overall, we were having a good season but having caught more in the first two weeks of the season than in the following six, the decline in production was frustrating. In addition, the seemingly constant battling with the weather was beginning to take a toll.

As the daylight waned, I was becoming a bit concerned about the weather. We still had four hours of running time to get to our destination, and the swells were topping 20 feet. The *Ballad*, weighted down by the full load of crab pots on her deck, was rolling hard with each wave. If she rolled too hard, we had the danger of the entire load shifting on deck, and the boat losing her stability and rolling over in the icy seas as the weight of the crab pots pulled her off center. The result would mean certain death for some, if not all, of the men aboard.

With the winds and seas increasing by the minute, the situation was quickly becoming serious. With each wave, the *Ballad* seemed to roll harder than ever, dipping her rails in the water and scooping up tons of water, further diminishing her stability as it sloshed around on deck. Then just as the water would finally empty itself, pouring from the 1'x3' freeing-ports that lined the rails at deck level every two feet, another wave would slam into the boat, laying her hard over once again as another load of water poured over the rails. With the roll getting more severe and the boat taking longer and longer to recover, I finally made the decision to dump our load of pots and heave to jogging into the huge seas, waiting for the storm to subside.

But a challenge soon presented itself. The pots onboard were rigged to fish shallower water and dumping them overboard where we were located could result in the entire load being lost. The weight of the pots sinking would pull the buoys under, stretching the lines to their limits. In order to get the pots off the boat where we could retrieve them, we had to venture into the shallower water. Shallower water meant bigger seas as the bottom of each wave met the rising sea bottom and pushed the whole mass of water ever higher until it would finally break upon the rocky cliffs that lined the coast.

By the time we reached the waters that were at the 20-fathom curve, just barely shallow enough to dump our gear, the seas were immense. At over 30 feet, their white foaming crests threatened to break at any moment, slamming broadside into the *Ballad*. My knuckles were white on the controls as I gave the command to my crew, "Don't worry about spacing. Just get 'em off the boat as fast as you can!"

The weight of the crab pots onboard and the size of the seas created a very dangerous situation. We were pushing things to the limit, and I struggled to keep the boat on course while the crew threw crab pots off both sides of the boat. We would have a challenge picking them up again because they were dumped in such a haphazard manner. What's more, we were dumping our gear onto a gravel seabed where chances were slim to none that we would catch any crab. But none of that mattered at that point in time. What *did* matter was getting the gear off the boat as quickly as possible and making our way offshore to the relative safety of deeper waters where, hopefully, the waves would not be breaking with such ferocity...I hoped.

In less than 30 minutes, the last pot went over the rail just as a huge breaker slammed into the starboard side of the *Ballad*, rolling her hard over with tons of icy cold water cascading across the deck and sweeping everything in its path over the side. Luckily, the guys on deck saw it coming and ran for cover where the upper deck hung over the main deck near the entrance to the galley. Quickly stripping off their soaking wet rain-gear, they made their way into the warm confines of the cabin as I turned the boat seaward to begin the slow jog out to deeper waters.

A low, ghostly howl started to reverberate through the boat permeated by high-pitched shrieks as the increasing winds whipped through the rigging holding the mast secure. We literally launched off each wave passing beneath us with a long freefall to the trough between it and the next. The howl of the wind in the rigging would suddenly become silent as the towering waves blocked the wind, only to be replaced by the crash of water slamming over the bow and into the windows of the wheelhouse.

The winds were now in excess of 50 knots, and the seas were fierce. I called out on all of the local VHF radio frequencies to find out if other boats were in the vicinity. Only silence met my radio calls. The realization sunk in that we were alone in one of the worst storms I had yet to experience aboard the *Ballad*. The updated weather forecast was now broadcasting hurricane force winds from the Northwest.

My mind whirled for a plan of action. The Coast Guard closed the entrance to both Grays Harbor and the Columbia River to all marine traffic due to the extreme danger presented by the mountainous breakers sweeping across the river bars guarding their mouths. The Strait of Juan de Fuca lay 60 miles directly north, and we were not in a position to run broadside in such heavy seas. My options came down to hanging on tight and battling it out with the storm.

My body ached with fatigue as I stood glued to the helm, throttling back as we reached the top of each wave then throttling ahead to keep from being pushed broadside or backward when the next wave appeared suddenly out of the darkness with the white crest glowing in the sodium lights atop the mast.

The crew spent the time in their bunks, using pillows, blankets and clothing to wedge themselves in as the boat fell from the peak of each wave. Occasionally Lane or Big D would come up to the wheelhouse (sometimes in one big step as the boat heaved them upward when we climbed yet another mountain of water) to ask if I wanted some relief. I was grateful for their offers, but due to the extreme sea conditions, I thanked them and silently said a prayer for their safety as they made their way back down the stairs to their coffin-like bunks below. If you have ever watched the reality show, *The Deadliest Catch*®, you get an idea of the tight living quarters these stocky, hard-working men must endure.

> *"I have set my rainbow in the clouds, and it will be the sign of a covenant between me and the earth."*
>
> *~Genesis 9:13~*

After 12 hours of bucking headlong into the seas, the darkness gave way to a light gray dawn, and the screaming winds diminished, taking the edge off the seas. The ghostly howl that accompanied us through the night was silenced, and instead of crashing through breaking walls of whitewater, the *Ballad* now rose and fell in a steady rhythm when we passed over the huge swells. During the night, we managed to make our way some forty miles offshore, and I was exhausted. My shoulders ached from standing at the helm all through the night, and the inside of the boat was a wreck. Anything that was on a shelf, a countertop or in the galley sink became airborne, and the floor was strewn with clothes, books, magazines and dishes.

The fierce winds diminished to what now seemed like a "comfortable" gale force and seas continued to subside, so I turned the boat on a southeasterly course towards the Columbia River. We wouldn't reach the river for another 12 hours, but the ride would be comfortable with the seas directly on our stern. By the time we arrived, the river bar would be open, and we would be able to make port in Warrenton for a hot meal, clean clothes and well-deserved rest.

As I turned the helm over to Lane, I crawled into my bunk, propping two pillows along side to keep me from rolling out. I lay looking out the windows to the mast, towering overhead reflecting on the fierce storm we came through, grateful for the unseen hand that shared the helm with me for so many hours. As my eyes closed, my last thoughts were of a beautiful bird soaring across the gray sea, swooping through the troughs and over the tops of the waves that only hours earlier promised destruction. A golden shaft of sunlight shining through from the heavens above lighted the bird's wingtips.

CHAPTER TEN
Daybreak

"You must listen to your own heart.
You can't be successful if you aren't happy with what you are doing."

~ Curtis Carlson ~

Save for the first two weeks of fishing, the rest of the season became a blur. Plagued by mechanical trouble and terrible weather throughout, each week came to resemble the one before as storm after storm followed the jet stream, tracking their way from the Bering Sea across thousands of miles of open ocean before lashing the Washington coast with high winds and heavy seas. We took an especially bad beating during the storm off Destruction Island.

With poor catches being reported throughout the fishing ports of Washington and Oregon, I decided to take advantage of a lull in the weather and hauled three full loads of gear back to port where they were now stacked in the gear shed in neat rows that towered twenty feet to the ceiling. After searching the grounds for lost gear, we returned with only 750 of the *Ballad's* original complement of 900 pots. At $100 apiece, I was not happy about it, but given the severity of the weather we faced, it was within the realm of acceptability.

Jolted back into the present by the slamming of a door in the cannery office and the accompanying rush of cold air, I looked down at the catch report lying on the desk in front of me with my hands deep in the pockets of my grimy sweatshirt. I was exhausted and wanted nothing more than a hot shower and a long nap in a big bed—one with clean, white sheets that would not require a death grip on the mattress to keep from being thrown out!

"Congratulations, you're number one!" David exclaimed, as he finished scanning the numbers on the report and stood up to offer his hand. "Second year in a row, too!"

"Thanks," I said quietly as I returned his handshake. Although relatively short in duration, the season had been one of the most difficult and challenging I faced in the eight years I was Captain of the *Ballad*. I was grateful for the efforts of my crew and proud of the fact that our perseverance paid off, but something was missing.

Searching for Answers

Returning to my home in Seattle, my time in the following weeks was spent resting and reflecting on the season, trying to figure out why I felt so empty in its wake. Somehow the sea took something from me—a vital part of what sustained me through so many years as a fisherman. I spent the better part of the last 18 years plying the cold waters of the North Pacific. I worked hard in nearly every fishery from the Bering Sea to the Oregon coast. During my years as a crewman, I played just as hard when ashore. I traveled the world between seasons, living a lifestyle many only dreamed of and had blown hundreds of thousands of dollars on toys while living in the fast lane. Through it all, I dreamed of becoming a Highliner.

I always was driven to go the extra mile and to do whatever it took to be the best as a fisherman. I took incredible risks, some stupid, and experienced my share of hardship, but still I drove ahead as if I had something to prove. I remembered screaming at storms at the top of my lungs, "Is that all you've got? Come on! I'll beat you!" as we slammed into oncoming seas. Yet the sea was merciful, and except for some very close calls, I was spared the same fate of the too many fishermen, including some friends, who were lost at sea. I did have something to prove. I wanted to be the best, to be respected and admired. And after taking command of the Ballad in 1990, I was just that. I learned well the ways of a Highliner, but my success as a Captain was only a salve.

I became a better man from the many hard lessons offered during that time and began to look inward as I worked to better myself. I turned off the money-spigot and started investing my hard-earned income wisely. More importantly, I invested in myself, reading hundreds of books on human behavior and personal development, attending trainings and seminars and earning certifications along the way. I learned many, many valuable lessons during my years as a fisherman as well as my studies on land. I became one of the most successful crab fishermen out of a fleet of thousands, yet I felt such emptiness.

"Purpose is the engine, the power that drives and directs our lives."

~John R. Noe~

As a fisherman, I gained the respect of my peers, appreciation of my crews and earned a substantial amount of money in the process, but my heart told me that my future lay on a different path. I was beginning to think that my future path was not that of a fisherman, and the time had come to venture forth in a new direction and apply what I learned using the God-given talents I was born with!

What exactly all this meant was still unknown, but I would take a season off and try out my land legs.

Showing off an 11-pound Kodiak king crab in 1982.
No shirt? Must've been a greenhorn thing…

Throwing the hook on the Mark I during Brown King Crab season at Attu Island in
1982. Peak winds during this storm exceeded 130 knots.

Shoveling a load of shrimp on the Laura in Port Bainbridge, 1985. Great group of guys, lots of fun and one of the easiest money making jobs I ever had.

Salmon seining on the Cape Spencer in Prince William Sound, 1986. Fun for a season and beautiful scenery, but I missed the rougher aspects of offshore fisheries.

*F/V Ballad leaving the docks on opening day of 1997
Dungeness Crab season loaded with 300 crab pots.*

*My friend Derek Ray at the helm of Dominion during Kodiak's Dungeness
Crab fishery in 1987. Derek later became one of the top Highliners in the
Bering Sea as captain of the Siberian Sea.*

*Big-D and Brian setting crab gear off the Ballad near Long Beach,
Washington during (unusually) calm weather circa 1992. The Washington
coast during winter can build enormous waves of 50+.*

*Eric relaxing on a full load of Dungeness crab on the Ballad.
This was not an uncommon load for the Ballad.*

The Ballad anchored in Lazy Bay taking a break from Kodiak's Dungeness fishery.
This was taken a week or so before we ran aground on Aiaktalik Island.

Not much elbow room for the boys while taking a break for dinner on the
Ballad during Dungeness crab season. Marty, Steve, Curtis, and Troy.

Nice pot of snow crab coming on the F/V Aleutian Ballad. I worked on this boat as a crewman and a captain at various times.

The deck and wheelhouse of the Aleutian Ballad covered in ice during the Bering Sea Opilio crab season.

The Aleutian Ballad during summer in Dutch Harbor getting ready for salmon tendering. Later retired from crabbing, the Aleutian Ballad's Deadliest Catch tours in Ketchikan, Alaska became one of the top cruise-ship excursions in the United States.

I am posing with a medium-sized halibut caught while shrimp fishing for Billy Wiley on the Laura in 1985.

Our feathered friends following the boat near the Simidi Islands in Alaska.
The birds were constant companions, even during storms. The only time a
flock wasn't around was 200+ miles off-shore.

Snake and Balls working up long-line gear on the Ballad near
the Island of Four Mountains during the Ballad's first long-line season.
Owner and my friend, David Lethin, at the helm.

The Highliner's Highliner, David Lethin, gaffing a halibut near Beaver Inlet, Unlaska Island during the Ballad's first long-line season. Seventy-two hours straight fishing, and we loaded the boat – the first of many such loads. "Welcome aboard boys!"

A peaceful morning greets me on the Ballad after a non-stop grind to fill the boat on our last trip. Little did I know two days later, we would be running for our lives across the North Pacific with a monster storm chasing right behind us.

SECTION II:

DANGER AT SEA

"The winners in life think constantly in terms of "I can," "I will," and "I am." Losers, on the other hand, concentrate on what they should have done or what they don't do."

~ Dennis Waitley ~

CHAPTER ELEVEN
Setting Course II

"It must be born in mind that the tragedy of life doesn't lie in not reaching your goal. The tragedy lies in having no goals to reach. It isn't a calamity to die with dreams unfulfilled, but it is a calamity to not dream. It is not a disgrace to reach for the stars, but it is a disgrace to have no stars to reach for. Not failure but low aim is a sin."

~Helmutt Schmidt~

"Hey, Marty! Where are Chief and Curtis?" I called out as I slammed the door to my truck and started walking towards the gear shed, shifting my baseball cap and playing catch with my keys as I went.

"Hey, Boss!" Marty replied. "They're inside measuring the buoy-line. Somebody got into it over the winter, and it's kind of messed up."

"Wow! Too bad. Whatcha' got going there?" I asked as I looked over the mountain of buoys he draped over six white, plastic totes, pallets and assorted boxes of gear packed onto the forty-foot trailer hitched to his truck. A cluster of bright, orange flags mounted atop a bundle of long aluminum poles stuck out the top of the pile. Twelve feet long, each pole was fitted with long, cylindrical buoys at their centers causing the bundle to bulge out slightly in the middle. Used to mark the ends of a longline set, a twenty-pound lead was bolted to the bottom of each pole that would hold the marker flags in a vertical position when in the water.

"Well, we've got 150 skates of halibut gear, 50 belted tubs, a bunch of anchors, enough buoys and flags for seven sets, 15,000 halibut hooks and 30,000 extra black cod hooks," Marty replied, listing off the mountain of supplies that we would need for the season. "We already loaded 150 skates of black cod gear and 100 tubs on the boat."

"Great!" I replied, still wondering if half the pile would fall off the trailer at the first turn on the way to the dock. Fishermen had a way of piling impossible amounts of gear on a truck or a trailer and then speeding down the road with the load swaying this way and that until finally reaching their destination, somehow without losing a thing—most of the time anyway. "Make sure that stuff's tied down good," I told Marty. I remembered losing 20 Dungeness pots off the back of the same, overloaded trailer years ago. Most scattered across the road in a jumbled pile, the tangle of lines and buoys spread all over the road creating a traffic hazard. Several more bounced off the small bridge, one landed in a small tree and the rest fell in the murky waters of the slough beneath. I chuckled to myself at the thought of climbing a tree to retrieve a crab pot.

We were gearing up the *Ballad* for our yearly trip to Alaska for the halibut and sablefish longline fisheries. After the grueling, storm lashed crab season a year and a half earlier, I had taken the following winter off to explore other options. During that time, I met my "dream girl," and we were engaged to be married in June. The emptiness was finally gone! The upcoming summer was to be my last as a commercial fisherman. I was looking forward to it with a mix of the familiar anticipation that always accompanied the beginning of a fishing season along with a desire to turn away from the sea and move ahead into the future that lay ahead for Lorraine and me.

Tossing a coil of crab line back and forth in a criss-cross pattern across the trailer, I helped Marty secure the load of gear to the trailer. After years of working together, we had the departure drill down to a science. One day would be to fit the hydraulic longline puller, outriggers and other deck gear; another to fit the shelter deck on the boat; and another to load the gear. On the last day, we would get groceries, load bait and fuel, and wrap up loose ends. Then, on the outgoing tide, we would be off.

"In all things, success depends upon preparation,
and without preparation,
there is sure to be failure."

~ Confucius ~

The shelter deck was always the most difficult and time consuming part. Looking like a giant aluminum box, 40 feet in length and 20 feet wide, it was bolted to the rails of the back deck. It completely enclosed the deck save for a ten-foot opening at the forward corner on the starboard side where the gear would be brought aboard when fishing. Inside, the walls were lined with racks to hold the tubs of longline gear. Another rack was mounted in the center of the deck just aft of the "table" where the crew would clean the catch before sliding them into the fish hold below. With fluorescent lights throughout, the result was a fully enclosed workspace that protected the crew from the brutal winds and icy seas that were so often a part of fishing Alaskan waters.

Longlining was a very labor-intensive fishery. Unlike the brute strength required for the crab fisheries, it required hours of detailed work, hauling, repairing and setting back the miles of ground line that made up each set. When the big, white-sided halibut came aboard, the work could be backbreaking with 50,000 pounds coming over the rail in 24 to 48 hours. But, the sheer beauty of the Alaskan coast always made the trip enjoyable. In addition, a $50,000 paycheck dangled like a carrot at the end of the three to four month season.

Gearing Up

As I turned the corner into the gear shed, I could see Chief and Curtis busily coiling lengths of line into a collection of brown, plastic garbage cans. Both of them were dressed in the "fisherman's uniform" of faded sweats and brown rubber boots topped off by threadbare baseball caps. They worked aboard the Highliner, *Ocean Ballad*, during the Bering Sea crab fisheries in the winter and worked with me on the Ballad during the summer months for several years. Two of the best crewmen I ever met, they had years of fishing experience between them and were solid, dependable professionals. To have them onboard made my job immeasurably easier.

"Hey, Smitty, how's it going?" Chief asked with a smile, as he saw me approach. He carried 230 pounds of muscle on a six-foot three-inch frame, had sharp features, long blond hair and had a penchant for riding in limousines in his wilder days. He had even been mistaken once for the model, Fabio, by hoards of teenage girls during a vacation in Southern California.

"Pretty darned good, Chief," I replied with a smile. "How goes the buoy line?"

"This is the last of it," he answered. "We've got enough line for four, 500-fathom sets, and it's all separated and marked in 20, 50 and 150-fathom coils. Curtis is just finishing up with the twenties now, and then we're done."

"Right on. Let's make sure we bring at least 10 coils of that new ground line as well, just in case we lose some buoy line or need to build any new gear."

"It's already on the boat," Curtis said as he finished the last of the buoy line. He tied the coil with a clove hitch and tossed it in the garbage can at his side. A man of few words, Curtis was one of those guys who carried a lean, athletic build well into his thirties without working out, making other guys feel old as a result. The long ash at the end of the ever-present cigar dangling from his mouth dropped off and cascaded down the front of his sweatshirt and into the garbage can as he stood up and stretched his arms. "What's the weather look like?" he asked.

"Pretty good, so far," I answered. "If the weather holds, we'll run up the outside of Vancouver Island and then duck inside after that."

The Inside Passage

The Inside Passage was an incredibly beautiful trip through the narrow, occasionally meandering waterways that lay between the countless islands dotting the coasts of British Columbia and Southeast Alaska. Bordered by towering peaks and endless, emerald-green forest, the cold, clear waters were teeming with marine life, and the sheer beauty of the trip made it a tremendously popular cruise destination. On any given day during the summer months, you could find up to three or four of the gleaming white cruise ships tied to the waterfront of the numerous small fishing towns that dotted the Passage. Rain or shine, their passengers would descend in hoards upon the tourist shops that welcomed them with open arms and cash registers that stood primed and ready.

Even though we enjoyed the beauty in the Inside Passage, I chose to travel through it for a more fundamental purpose: the weather. The mountainous islands along the coast helped to keep the frequent gales of the North Pacific at bay, providing for a peaceful and relaxing ride in the calm waters of the Passage. Nevertheless, after reaching the border between Alaska and British Columbia, we would turn the boat due west, leave its protected waters, pass through Dixon Entrance, and head out into the wide-open expanse of the Gulf of Alaska that lay beyond.

We left Warrenton two days later on the outgoing tide. The Columbia River bar was smooth and flat, and after swinging around the last of the buoys marking the approach to the river, I set course for Cape Scott, 350 miles to the north-northwest. The evening was beautiful as the sun slid slowly over the western horizon, casting streaks of red-gold rays upon the calm waters ahead. A pod of porpoises rode our bow wave as if guiding us out to sea.

We reached Cape Scott after 36 hours, and I briefly toyed with the idea of running straight across from there. But Environment Canada in Alert Bay broadcast gale warnings for the outside waters, so after rounding the cape, we ducked inside. Our days slowly blended into a monotonous cycle of eating, reading and sleeping. We took turns standing watch as the *Ballad* wound her way northward through the labyrinth of waters that made up the Inside Passage. As always, the trip was beautiful with the scenery becoming more rugged and wild as day turned to night, and the miles rolled by.

Keep On Keepin' On

With the gear work done, we had little to keep us occupied, and by the fourth day, the novelty of the trip begun to wear off. The boredom mariners come to know so well set in, and it was with some relief that we finally broke out of the confines of the Inside Passage, passing through the widening expanse of Dixon Entrance and out into the cold, slate-gray waters of the Gulf of Alaska. After setting course for the fishing grounds south of Seward 600 miles to the northwest, I climbed back into my chair, put my feet up on the dash and took a sip of coffee. I looked far off to the horizon ahead, "Two more days," I thought, "and then the fun will begin."

I always enjoyed the slow transition from daylight to dark—in good weather at least. This was a peaceful time as darkness settled over the northern waters with the sodium lights on the mast high above casting a pale, golden glow on the waters highlighting a flock of birds swooping and diving over the waves. The single-sideband radio would liven up as the darkness set in as well. The daylight static softened, and the voices of fishermen hundreds of miles away suddenly became sharp and clear as they called in catch reports and shared weather observations.

"Hey Smitty, what's Rush got to say?" I looked over to see Chief settling into his usual spot on the wide bench on the port side of the wheelhouse.

"I dunno, let's find out," I replied, as I reached for the radio. Several years earlier, I discovered we could pick KSFO Talk Radio out of San Francisco during the evenings, and ever since then, Rush Limbaugh's ranting became a part of our nightly routine. Later that summer, as we crossed back and forth across the gulf to deliver loads of halibut in Bellingham, Washington, we were glued to the radio as President Clinton's impeachment hearings progressed.

Rush was in fine form that evening, followed by the news and Art Bell's strange musings on alien abductions on Coast-to-Coast AM. By midnight, we had enough, and Chief slid down the wheelhouse stairs in search of his bunk. I turned the radio down, checked the coordinates on the GPS, walked to the chart table, and plotted our position on the course line I drew across the chart. Next, I wrote a brief entry into my logbook including position, course (true and magnetic), weather (winds SE 15 knots, seas 6 feet), and anything of consequence that happened since my last entry six hours earlier (switched from aft fuel tanks to forward, boat trim and riding smoothly). Then, with a last look at the radar, I went downstairs and woke Marty to stand watch.

Ten minutes later, Marty appeared in the wheelhouse. The sharp sound of a soda can being opened announced his arrival followed by his usual, "Hey, Boss!" Looking back, I could see him bent over the chart table, checking our position with what was showing on the GPS. I slipped out of my chair and folded down the bench on the port side, revealing my bunk below as Marty completed the same examination of the navigational electronics that I did just moments before.

"Keep on keepin' on Marty," I said as I crawled into my bunk and pulled the sleeping bag up to my chin. "Keep an eye out for ships, and give 'em plenty of room," I said, reminding him that oil tankers might be encountered, making their way south from Valdez. With the crew I had onboard, I rarely bothered to write up a watch list when running in the open sea and had not done so that evening. The three of them were no strangers to the sea; their navigational skills were sharp, boat handling skills good and all were experienced as either a full-time or a relief Captain. We had been across these waters many times together, and they had their individual watch routines down pat. I looked over at Marty one last time, pulled my sleeping bag up even tighter and opened the Luis L'Amour novel I was working on. Ten minutes later, I was asleep, the book having slipped out of my hands, landing on the floor alongside my bunk.

"I know God will not give me anything I can't handle.
I just wish He didn't trust me so much."

~Mother Teresa~

The stagecoach swayed to-and-fro as it wound its way between the giant saguaro cactus' and immense pillars of sandstone that adorned the southwestern desert. We were still six hours out of Santa Fe, and the road was beginning to deteriorate rapidly. I leaned against the polished wooden railing, peering out the window, and the coach lurched sharply when one of the wheels fell into a hole. As the coach started to fall, I found myself airborne and reached out for... nothing.

Welcome Back, Boys!

"Oooof!" The air was punched from my lungs when I landed hard, followed by a moment of confusion as I opened my eyes. Instead of the dry desert of a fading dream, I saw Chief sitting in the Captain's chair of the *Ballad*, holding a blue, plastic cereal bowl tight against the ceiling above him. "What're you doing!?" I asked, slightly annoyed by my rude awakening as we slammed into yet another wave.

"Man! You wouldn't believe it!" Chief exclaimed in amazement. "I was sitting here peacefully eating my Frosted Flakes® when we flew off a wave.

Everything in my bowl—cereal, milk, *everything*—came out in a large column about two feet high, and I figured the only thing I could do was trap it against the ceiling!" I watched in amazement as he carefully lowered the bowl, leaving a milk ring on the ceiling above him.

Throwing my sleeping bag aside, I swung my legs over the edge of my bunk and started to stand up, only to be thrown back on my bunk when the boat launched off yet another wave. My timing was better the second time, and soon I was looking out at angry, 15-foot seas adorned with white stripes of spindrift, standing out in glaring contrast to the gray water in the bright light of early morning.

"Must be the Gulf's way of saying 'Welcome back, Boys'," I muttered bouncing over to the chart table to check our position. After listening to the weather forecast the night before, I knew a low-pressure system was moving its way across the Gulf of Alaska, but I did not expect to encounter much wind until the next day. By then, we would have been 24 hours and 240 miles closer to our destination. Still not quite awake and feeling a bit grumpy, I slid down the stairs to the galley, leaving Chief at the wheel.

The coffee machine was empty. "Great," I said sarcastically as I placed Mr. Coffee's® water dispenser in the galley sink and turned on the faucet. A second later, I was airborne again when the Ballad launched off another enormous wave. Pushed by the momentum of the boat, the water from the faucet hesitated slightly before turning 90-degees, where the now horizontal flow of water flooded the countertop before falling back to its rightful vertical position. Landing with a thud, I reached out for the stove to steady myself, and the water on the counter sloshed onto the floor soaking my socks. The day was definitely not off to a good start.

After filling the coffee machine, I donned the hearing-protection earmuffs hung on the fire extinguisher near the door to the stateroom, opened the door to the engine room and bounced my way down the ladder, banging my head on the top step as I went. After walking around the engines checking for oil leaks or anything else that might spell trouble, I made my way aft to check the fuel system water traps before returning to the center of the engine room. I sat down on the aluminum casing covering the small auxiliary engine and rubbed the bruise on my forehead. Far down below the wheelhouse, the bucking and pitching was not so violent, and the heat of the metal floor felt good on my wet feet. I learned years ago that the sound and vibration told more about how an engine was running than anything else and every so often, I would just sit and listen. But today, I mostly wanted to escape the rough ride that jolted me out of bed and dry out my socks.

Five minutes later, my socks dry, I climbed back up the ladder and stepped into the galley. "Aw, ya gotta be kidding!" The water that spilled sloshed back and forth, leaving zigzagging streamers of water across the floor. My socks were wet again. Resigned to breaking into my stash of clean socks several days sooner than expected, I poured myself a cup of coffee and carefully made my way over to the wheelhouse stairs. With careful timing, I raised and lowered the cup in time with the rise and fall of the boat, managing to keep its contents where it belonged. Just as I reached the top stair, the boat dropped away once again, splashing burning, hot coffee down the front of my sweats.

"Hey, Chief!" I hollered "Do ya think you can find any *more* holes in the road?" Chief looked back and started to laugh when I handed him the half-full coffee cup to hold while I changed clothes. "I am not having a good start to my morning. Wake me up in an hour, and I'll try again." And with that, I climbed back into my bunk, wedged myself against the wall with my pillows and pulled my sleeping bag over my head. Over the thrum of the engines and the crash of the waves, I could hear Chief laughing at me as the boat dropped off another wave, and I was airborne once again.

CHAPTER TWELVE
A Change of Plans

"You are free to choose, but the choices you make today will determine what you will have, be and do in the tomorrow of your life."

-Zig Ziglar-

"We're on 'em now boys!" I shouted across the deck as I pulled my gaff from the halibut I just brought aboard, spun around and slammed it home just as another fish broke the water seconds later. The puller behind me creaked and groaned with the ground line heavy with fish. The "kill-bin" was full, and fish begun to spill out into the deck checker alongside, which was beginning to fill rapidly.

A Better Start

Only twelve hours into the season, Chief was already covered with fish slime and blood. He attacked each fish with a razor sharp knife, throwing the gills and entrails overboard before scraping the body cavity clean, and slid them into the fish hold where Marty was busy packing them in ice. Standing by the puller, Curtis was a flurry of activity, repairing broken gangions and bent hooks as he backhauled the gear for another set. One after another of the lively, white-sided flatfish came over the rail. With most of the fish ranging from 30 to 60 pounds, I called them "School fish." They weren't giants by any means, but the steady volume and consistency in size told me an abundance of fish gathered on the gravel beds 150 fathoms below.

After a half-day of bucking into heavy seas (starting the morning I was awakened so rudely), the weather gradually swung around, first to the southwest then south before finally settling in to a strong, southeasterly gale as the low pushed its way across the Gulf. After chewing up the miles at 11 knots, our arrival on the fishing grounds was greeted by diminishing winds and broken clouds with the "midnight sun" casting its welcome rays upon the cold northern waters.

We started our trip 50 miles offshore on the eastern corner of the Seward Gully, an enormous submarine canyon where the broad continental shelf bordering South-Central Alaska turns southward before sweeping around Kodiak Island 200 miles to the southwest and along the Alaska Peninsula. With only two boats appearing on the radar 20 miles to the east, the fishing grounds were wide open. After six hours of zigzagging back and forth along the edge and mapping the bottom contours on the plotter, we splashed four five-tub test sets in an effort to find the fish. The first two yielded little, offering only a handful of halibut and a smattering of cod, but the last two had been right on the money. We promptly set out 12 miles of ground line in four 25-tub sets in neat, parallel rows along the bank with one mile of spacing between them.

"The best morale exists when you rarely hear the word mentioned. When you hear a lot of talk about morale, it's usually very poor."

~Dwight D. Eisenhower~

"How's it going, Chief?" I yelled out as another 30-pounder came over the rail, its tail beating furiously in an effort to break free.

"Woo-hoo! Keep 'em comin' Smitty!" he answered as he threw another fish up on the table. He was an excellent butcher, but as I looked over at the pile of fish building up behind him, it was obvious that the increasing volume of fish was beginning to overwhelm him.

"Hey, Curtis! Give Chief a hand, will ya?"

"Roger!" Curtis replied as he tossed the tub of gear he was working on into the rack behind him, picked up a gaff and threw three fish up on the table for cleaning. Turning back to the rail, I gaffed fish after fish as the ground line pulled them up through the cold, dark waters in ever-increasing numbers.

Four hours later, I stood at the rail and surveyed the scene behind me. The buoy line marking the end of our fourth set sped through the puller, piling up in the garbage below. The deck looked like Jack the Ripper had made a visit. Entrails that had not made it over the side were hanging from the tub racks, and Chief and Curtis were blood splattered, painted red from head to toe with their legs twisted at odd angles, trapped against the table by the weight of the halibut covering the deck three feet deep. Tubs of gear that needed backhauling were stacked haphazardly along the port side, and with each roll of the boat, they swayed dangerously, threatening to fall over into a giant tangle of gray, ground line and shiny hooks that would take hours to sort out.

After hauling the last of the buoy line, I unclipped the flag and ran upstairs to set it in its cradle with the others. A quick scan of the horizon still showed no other boats in the vicinity. I slid down the ladder to the deck below, pulled on my raincoat and stepped into the pile of fish to lend a hand. "If this keeps up, we'll be done by tomorrow afternoon!" I announced, as I tossed a fish up on the table.

"Woo-hoo." Chief answered, with far less enthusiasm to his voice than he held six hours earlier. Curtis said nothing. I knew well the focused intensity that descended over them, and the lack of response was nothing to worry about. Butchering halibut is backbreaking work, and they were at it for over 16 hours, non-stop. Gloves become tattered remnants of what they had once been, and hands begin to ache as the tendons tighten up, screaming in protest at their overuse. Soaked from head to toe in fish slime, blood and sweat, shoulders and backs become sore from struggling with thousands of pounds of the enormous fish. Eyes begin to itch, faces become unemotional through blood-spattered masks, and the butcher puts his body on autopilot to retreat into the daydreams that reside in the recesses of his mind. As the show *The Deadliest Catch*® has proven, not everyone is cut out to be a fisherman.

After another two hours, the deck was finally cleared of fish, but with 40 tubs of gear to backhaul and 100 to bait, the work would continue for another eight hours. "No rest for the wicked," I thought as I peered into the fish hold to see how Marty was progressing. "How ya doin' down there, Marty?"

"Hey, Boss! I got the front six bins full to the ceiling. This middle bin I'm standing on's full, and as soon as I get this ice moved, it looks like I'll have enough to fill this port side bin about half-full," he said cheerfully, pointing to the bin full of ice at his feet. Ever the optimist, he did not have time for that focused intensity stuff… at least not for another few hours anyway. Marty was a slime ball. Literally. Crawling around on his belly in order to stuff fish into the forward reaches of the hold, he became covered in the grayish-red, gooey fish slime that covered the fish. It was now even dripping off the ceiling. His face was covered in neon hues of grease paint in order to prevent the slime from dripping off the bill of his baseball cap and into his face. His raingear was completely soaked.

"Yeah, OK," I said, barely able to keep from laughing at his appearance. "Go as fast as you can. We gotta get this gear backhauled and into the water as soon as we can." Thankful I did not have *his* job, I turned away from the hatch, picked up a tub and worked my way through the 600-feet of tangled ground line inside.

An Endless Summer

Berthing the gear slightly to the east, we set out four more strings during the soft, subtle glow of pre-dawn, wolfed down our first meal in over 24 hours and collapsed into our bunks for a four-hour nap. By nine-o'clock, the puller was turning once again, the line creaking and popping under the heavy load as fish after fish were brought over the rail.

After another twelve hours of non-stop hauling, I turned the boat away from the edge and set course for Homer, 150 miles to the northwest with our fish holds stuffed with 50,000 pounds of clean, fresh halibut.

The fish came quickly and easily, and our spirits were high with thoughts of a fat paycheck waiting at the end of a relatively short season dancing in our heads. Upon arriving in Homer, gray clouds of misfortune were looming on the horizon. The overall quota of halibut, established by the International Halibut Commission for Alaskan waters, had been increased prior to the season, and the anticipated glut of the halibut on the market had driven prices down to $1.95, far less than the $2.40 we expected. Worse yet, the prices were expected to continue to fall throughout the summer, with rumors of $1.20 or less as the season progressed. If that happened, our earnings would be cut in half.

The time came to "turn and burn", staying in town only long enough to offload our catch, get fuel, fresh bait and groceries, then cast off the lines in a mad scramble to catch as much of our quota as possible before the price bottomed out. With that thought in mind, I dispatched Marty to pick up fresh groceries. I then walked off the dock and across the gravel road to the Auction Block. After ordering another 6,000 pounds of squid bait, I made a quick call to several fish buyers in Seattle who confirmed the bad news I heard in Homer. "Easy come, easy go," I muttered in disgust as I hung up the phone. I walked outside into the cold drizzle to hunt down a couple of local fish buyers to see if they could offer a better price. Two "sorry can't help ya's" and one promising conversation later, I sat down in the phone booth across from the unloading dock and dialed David's number to fill him in.

"Hello!" He answered, on the first ring.

"David, this is Steve."

"Hey, where ya at? What's the good news?"

"We got into Homer late last night, and we're offloading now. We should have around 50,000 pounds, but the price we're getting is definitely *not* good news. We're looking at a buck-ninety."

"Yeah, I see… That's not good news. Looks like you better start bringing 'em south for the higher price," he said, referring to the extra fifty-cents we could make on a delivery to Bellingham, Washington.

"Well, I got a commitment from one of the buyers here in town to hold the black cod price at three-fifteen a pound for the next two weeks. That's ten-cents higher than anybody else is paying, and we were starting to get into the black cod pretty good on the deep ends of our sets," I said, as I laid out my plan. "I know those halibut are still there, too, and if we turn and burn back to the same spot, we'll get all of our black cod plus area 3A halibut quotas caught in the next two weeks. Then, we can start working on the quota out west."

David was leaning toward the higher price offered in Bellingham, and we discussed our options for another ten minutes before he rendered his verdict. Hanging up the phone, I zipped up my coat and pulled my baseball cap down tight before walking back across the road and out onto the dock to let my crew know what was up.

Seek First to Understand Then to Be Understood

"What!? You gotta be kidding me!"

"Nope. Wish I was, but that's the deal. Bring as much fish as we can to Bellingham," I said with a shrug. "I don't like it any more than you guys do, but the decision's been made. Let's get things cleaned up and get out of here." I turned and climbed down the long ladder from the dock to the boat 30 feet below. Not only were we looking at a substantial loss in earnings, but our three-month season just doubled in length. Those with wives (or in my case, fiancée) would have to break the bad news about the extended season, which would, undoubtedly, mess up personal plans.

Before the season was over, we would make the six-day transit across the Gulf of Alaska seven more times with over 42 days at sea and virtually nothing to do but sleep and read. We called it "The Endless Summer;" the days became weeks, and the weeks rolled into months, becoming a test of both patience and perseverance as the price plummeted. Our frustration intensified as our first two deliveries in Bellingham were met with the very same price that we would have received in Homer, just one week before.

Finally, with great relief, we turned our attention to the westward areas along the Alaska Peninsula and Aleutian Islands. Most of *that* fish would be delivered in Homer.

CHAPTER THIRTEEN
Perseverance III

"To succeed, we must have the will to succeed; we must have stamina, determination, backbone, perseverance, self-reliance and faith."

~B.C. Forbes~

During my years working as a crewman aboard the Ballad, I learned volumes about what it takes to be a Highliner, and the lesson about perseverance was one we enjoyed again and again. By its very nature, commercial fishing is an industry where success and failure often result from a man's ability to learn from misfortune, apply knowledge gained and pursue yet another opportunity for success.

Many things are beyond the control of a fisherman as he attempts to load his boat. The power of the sea is immense; the weather can change in a matter of hours from flat calm to raging seas driven by gale-force winds that fill the air with stinging salt-spray. All the while, he's in pursuit of fish that he can't even see because they are hidden in the cold, dark depths of the ocean. "Fish have tails…," he may mutter to himself, as he pulls up an empty set from the very place that, hours before, yielded an enormous catch. The difference between success and failure most often is the ability to learn from past failures and make yet another set.

Fishing Derbies

Starting in the mid 1980's and continuing into the early 1990's, another variable came into play for the fishermen participating in the Pacific Halibut fishery in Alaska and Western Canada. With the sheer volume of fish to be caught, the halibut fishery was becoming quite lucrative during a time when other fisheries were in decline due to changes in the ocean environment, including over-fishing. As a result, ever-greater numbers of boats were joining the fleet, making it necessary to manage the fishery by holding a series of short "openers" lasting from 24 to 48 hours throughout the summer months. With thousands of boats crowding the fishing grounds competing for fish, these openers soon came to be called "fishing derbies", and indeed that's what they were.

With the potential for a boat to catch and deliver in excess of $75,000 worth of fish during one 24-hour derby, the competition was fierce. Crewmen stood to earn up to $10,000 in a single day of fishing with the skippers and boat owners earning even more. With high-stakes on the table, boats crowded onto the fishing grounds in ever-increasing numbers, laying their longlines this way and that hoping to land their gear on the "mother-lode," and filling their holds with the big, heavy, white-sided halibut. All the while, they attempted to keep their gear from tangling with that of the fishermen nearby. Tempers would flare as the vessels jostled for position, each trying to outguess the other as to the best place to set with Captains and crew working around the clock without stopping for either rest or a meal. In the end when the derby was over, the boats would set course back to port, some of them celebrating their good fortune while others went home struggling to find meaning in a season of failure.

Of course, we had the weather to contend with as well. Because many of the vessels participating in the fishery counted their catch of halibut as a substantial portion of their yearly income, the choice to venture out in the storm-tossed waters was for many not a choice at all. Too often boats and men were lost to the sea during the derby days, foundering in the heavy seas, decks overloaded with too much of a good thing and halibut spilling over the rails back into the water.

Most of all, the derbies were an exercise in perseverance. By the time the season would close, Captains and crew were nearing physical exhaustion due to heavy work and a non-stop schedule. Backs were sore and arms cramped from lifting, cleaning and stowing the tens of thousands of pounds of fish aboard. For some of these boats, success for the opener would come out of sheer luck…their gear landing in the midst of an enormous school of fish with little competition nearby to stifle their efforts. For most, success during the opener lay with a continual turnover of gear, hauling and setting as many hooks as possible in the short time allotted. Discouragement was always at hand, ready to offer its promise of failure to those who would succumb to the temptation of stopping to rest before the end of the day.

Many a boat would leave port for a halibut derby, the crew dreaming together as they worked to ready the gear. Statements like, "Wouldn't it be great if we filled the boat this time?" or "I sure hope we land on 'em this time," might be heard as the boat bucked into the seas towards the fishing grounds offshore.

Gotta Have Attitude

Soon after signing on as a crewman aboard the Ballad, I noticed a different attitude that prevailed, and indeed it was an attitude that was present aboard all of the boats in the fleet that enjoyed consistent success. Instead of hoping we would succeed, it was expected, and instead of dreaming about success, the crew would spend much of their time talking about what they would do with the profits that were sure to come. David's enthusiasm and confidence was infectious, mirrored by the crew, regardless of the success or failure of the moment.

No matter how much we caught on the previous set, his response always seemed to be the same…to push ahead harder than ever. If we hauled a set that was full of fish, his attitude would be "Now we know where they are! Let's give it to 'em boys!" If we hauled a set that was empty, his attitude would shift slightly to "Now we know where they aren't! They must be over there. Let's give it to 'em boys!" And away we would go, charging full speed ahead! As we set and hauled our gear as fast as possible, we held the possibility of failure at bay with a burning desire to be one of the top-producers and kept the faith, *knowing beyond any doubt* that we would end the season with a boatload of fish.

This driving determination to be a Highliner that David displayed was revealed to me during my first year as a crewman aboard the *Ballad* during a Dungeness crab season off the coast of Washington State. He was upset that he slept four hours instead of two after working 72-hours straight without rest. Having been drifting well offshore during his nap and out of any danger, we suggested that halfway through a six-month season, and having caught over $1 million worth of crab in the preceding months that perhaps a bit of rest was not such a bad thing…especially considering we were the top-producing boat in the fleet, and we had no competition in sight. He looked at us with a twinkle in his eye and said, "Yeah, but while we were sleeping, somebody else was catching!" and with that, he bounded up the stairs to the wheelhouse.

Perseverance Pays Off

I remembered a season 11 years earlier aboard the *Ballad* as the darkness of night yielded to the soft glow of approaching daylight and morning dawned over the fishing grounds of the Albatross Bank, 90 miles off the coast of Kodiak Island. With nine hours left until the close of the halibut "derby," we caught just over 25,000 pounds of fish, far shy of the 60,000 pounds that the boat could hold when full. The truth in the old saying that "fish have tails…" seemed to be evident as every set we hauled so far was mediocre at best, with only the shallowest end of each set producing any sizeable catch. We had one set left in the water to haul and two sets on board that were baited and ready to go. Requiring two and a half hours to haul each longline, we would be racing down to the wire to set and haul all of our gear.

Regulations required that at 12:00 p.m. when the season officially closed, any boats that still had gear in the water were to stop fishing, abandon any gear they left in the water and set a course for town to unload. The Coast Guard would be flying C-130 airplanes across the expanses of ocean to help the cutters on station to enforce these regulations. Getting caught fishing after the season closed would not only risk seizure of the entire catch and a hefty fine, but it would also invite derision and ridicule by the other fishermen in the fleet. We had our work cut out for us, and time was ticking away.

"Let 'er go!" came the command over the loudhailer as we set the last of our gear. The hooks pulled off the tubs with a steady "tick, tick, tick" punctuated by a loud "pop!" whenever one got hung up as it was pulled off the stern. The seas had steadily grown worse throughout the night and were now running at 15 feet, and the morning dawn was greeted by a full gale blowing from the southeast at forty knots.

With the worsening weather and fatigue beginning to gnaw at our minds, we worked even harder to ensure we tied each knot correctly and each tub was prepared carefully before being set off the stern.

With the boat charging ahead in the rough seas at eight knots, all eyes were on the hooks as Curtis rotated the tub, the hooks continuing their cadence of "tick, tick, tick." If a hook were to flip out of place and catch on him when he was setting the gear, he could be severely injured or killed as the hook would tear through his skin or pull him overboard. A seasoned crewman and gifted with lighting fast reflexes, Curtis soon had the gear safely in the water to begin its long, slow drift before finally settling on the hard, rocky bottom 800 feet below.

With three sets to haul and under the gun, the atmosphere on the back deck was crackling with intense expectation as the first of the ground lines started to come aboard, hauled from the depths by the gigantic power block mounted on the port side. We didn't need to look at the empty hooks coming aboard to know that it would not be a good set. The ground line was quiet as it was spooled aboard, indicating a light load on the line below.

"This one's too deep," David announced as he turned up the speed of the hauler. "We'll get 'em on the two we just set, though. The fish are up on the bank in about 130 fathoms."

In just under two hours, we finished the set and caught only 4,000 pounds. Our total for the opener was just under half what we could hold. The success or failure of our season lay with the last two sets we made, and with six hours to the close of the season, time was running out. The Ballad rolled hard as we ran wide open in the trough, the seas slamming hard into the starboard side, filling the deck with spray.

Twenty minutes later as we pulled in the flag that marked the beginning of the set, the crew was silent. If this set were empty, it would be the first time the Ballad ever caught less than 50,000 pounds in any halibut season. Caught up with our work, we could do nothing but wait as the ground line once again was hauled up from the ocean floor.

"Welcome aboard!" David hollered as he brought the first halibut of the set over the rail. "Welcome aboard!"

Suddenly, the ground line got tight. The quiet rolling of gears was replaced with a popping and squealing as the hauler strained under the increasingly heavy load. Curtis and I exchanged glances with the change in sound. It could only mean one of two things: either the line was heavy with fish, or it was hung up on a rock outcropping on the seafloor far below.

"Welcome aboard!" David called as yet another fish came over the rail, "Comin' like grapes. Welcome aboard!"

The deck came to life as fish after fish came over the rail. With most of us having worked together as a crew for several years, we sprang into action like a well-oiled machine. Heaving the large white-sided fish up on the table for cleaning before pitching them down into the hold to be packed in ice, we kept up fairly well for the first twenty minutes, but soon the sheer volume of fish coming aboard took its toll. The fish started to pile up on deck, coming aboard faster than we could clean them with the arrival of every tenth fish or so heralded by David's ever present, "Welcome aboard!"

By the end of the set, we put 10,000 pounds of fish down in the hold, and we were still knee deep in fish. If the next set was anything like this one had been, then our season was saved!

"Where'd you put the other set?" I asked, as David was removing his raingear.

"Right over there," he said, "Same depth as this one only the bottom looked better. Get those fish down as quick as you can. The next set should be better, and we gotta keep moving!" Then with a wink, he bounced up the stairs to the wheelhouse and set course for our last set.

Three hours later, having finished hauling our last set with just minutes to spare before the end of the season, the *Ballad* was holding position, jogging at slow speed head on into the seas as we struggled to clean and stow the immense volume of fish that had been brought aboard. We would need another two hours to secure the deck, and then we could set course for town. With our fish holds full, we would have an additional 5,000 pounds of fish stacked white-side up in the middle of the deck.

Our spirits were high as we took off our raingear and went inside for a well-earned meal. The word on the radio was that the price at the dock would be around $1.20, the highest offered so far that season. With an estimated 65,000 pounds of halibut onboard, each crewman would earn just over $7,000 for a twenty-four hour season. A good payday to be sure, but more importantly, we kept moving ahead, even when all signs pointed to failure. We stuck with it and persevered, finding success in the last moments of the season.

As I lay in my bunk with sleep closing in, the frustration of the previous night vanished. We were Highliners! With that, I drifted off to sleep hearing

David up in the wheelhouse calling the *Sea Valley II*, our partner boat, fading in my mind, "Hey Grandpa! Ya got this one on?"

CHAPTER FOURTEEN
Lessons in Leadership

*"The world of the 90's and beyond will not belong to managers
or those who make the numbers dance, as we used to say, or
those who are conversant with all the business and jargon we use to sound
smart. The world will belong to passionate and driven leaders-
people who not only have an enormous amount of energy
but can energize those whom they lead."*

~Jack Welch~

I looked over at Curtis as he came up the wheelhouse stairs.

"We quit!" he remarked, sitting down in the extra seat on the port side.

"You what?" I asked.

"We quit. We're done!"

"I see..." I replied, "Do you have ninety tubs ready to go?"

"Nope. We only baited fifty," came the reply.

At this point, my Captain's Ego checked in. "Why did you only bait fifty tubs when I wanted ninety?" I said to Curtis in my best Captain's Voice. After all, I was the Captain, and we had a boatload of fish to catch in a limited amount of time. Bad weather kept much of the longline fleet in port, and the resulting decline in volume of fish moving onto the fresh market drove the dock prices higher.

The waters of the Shelikof Strait that separates Kodiak Island from the Alaska Peninsula flows both northeast and southwest, and Cook Inlet breathes immeasurable volumes in and out with the changing of the tides. Located where the tidal waters from the Shelikof Strait sweep around the south end of Kodiak to pour across the wide continental shelf, Chirikof Island is a small, desolate chunk of black rock some 50 miles offshore with towering cliffs topped with green tundra. The area around it was known as a "blow hole" because the weather always seemed to be worse there than the surrounding areas. The banks along the edge of the shelf where the sea bottom plunged some 20,000 feet down into the bottomless depths of the Aleutian Trench yielded rich fishing, and in my mind, the trade off was worth it. With a brief lull in the weather forecast for the area, I wanted to hit it hard and get a quick trip in, but with another low working its way westward across the Aleutian chain, the window of opportunity in which to do so was short.

My mind raced. What with the weather, tides and the multitude of other things a fishing boat Captain must contend with, who were these guys to add to my stress level by so blatantly disregarding my direction? I specifically asked for ninety tubs of gear to be ready to set when we reached the fishing grounds.

"Well, we figured that when we got to the grounds, you'd want to set and haul three or four five-tub test strings to locate the fish before setting any long strings," Curtis replied, "That's what we've always done for the last three years. So what's the plan?"

"That is the plan," I replied.

"Great! The test strings are short enough that we'll only need one guy to dress fish, and the rest of us can backhaul gear. If we don't find fish here, the bait won't go bad. If there are, we'll start baiting as they come aboard. By the time we're done hauling the testers, we'll be ready to set as many as you want."

Leaders Lead People

Who were these guys? They were top-notch crewmen with over 50 years combined fishing experience between the four of them, and they were well aware that having ninety tubs ready to fish was not our goal. The real goal was to catch 50,000 pounds of halibut as quickly as possible. They had fished with me for years, and they all knew my fishing style. They knew their responsibilities, and they knew their capabilities as a team.

As Curtis disappeared down the stairs, I sat back and silently reflected on a piece of advice given to me several years before, at a different time and in a different place, but just as applicable at that moment.

My crew spent the four weeks prior to a Dungeness crab season off the Washington coast preparing our fishing gear for the upcoming opener. I walked into the 6,000 square-foot storage warehouse to check on their progress and lend a hand. The floor was strewn with piles of freshly spliced crab line, racks of bullet shaped buoys hanging from overhead hooks so the fresh coats of bright orange paint could dry and piles of round steel crab pots wrapped in black rubber, covered with stainless steel mesh.

I turned a pot over and repaired a hole in the mesh. I watched the guys work taking note of the system they had in place to ensure that all of the gear was checked, any needed repairs made and everything stowed for the long haul on a trailer to the cannery dock where it all would be loaded aboard the *Ballad*. From my view, they could speed up the whole process if they made some changes in how they arranged their work area in the cluttered gear shed. As I began to move gear and tools around to make what I saw as well-needed changes, I indicated to my crew what changes I thought should be made— I unwittingly stepped out of the role of a leader and into that of a manager.

As soon as I re-arranged the work area in the gear shed, my crew started to grumble. They worked together for three weeks, were on schedule, and the gear was being well taken care of. They developed a system that worked for them and resented the fact that I simply walked in and started to change things without regard to what worked for them.

As I lifted another bundle of lines to put it in a "better" place, I looked over to see David, the owner of the Ballad, standing in the doorway calmly watching the whole process unfold. "Hey, look at this! Gear everywhere! Ya think you guys got enough pots in here?" he asked with a sparkle in his eyes. "Marty! Go long!" And with that, he picked up one of the bullet shaped buoys and sent it flying in a perfect, spiraling arc as Marty ran through the stacks of crab pots like defenders on a football field in an attempt to catch the buoy before it crashed against the back wall. In less than 30 seconds, he took the focus off the "system" and put it back on the people. "Hey, Smitty," he called over, using my nickname. "Let's go for a ride down to the cannery. There's some gear I wanna check out."

"Yeah OK," I agreed and followed him out the door and into the damp cold of the ever-present winter rains. We crossed the muddy parking lot and climbed into his full-size Chevy Suburban.

Climbing into the driver's side, David started the engine, turned the heater switch on to ward off the chill and leaned back in his seat. "That's really not your style," he said, looking over at me. "I know you're getting wound tighter as the season opener approaches, but you need to cut those guys some slack and let'em do things their way. Don't micro-manage them. They're good, competent crewmen, and they know what they're doing. Just let 'em know what the goal is, point 'em in the right direction and then leave 'em alone and let 'em do their job… Now let's go get some lunch, and then we'll head down to the cannery to look at that gear."

David was right. Micro-management wasn't my style; I had never seen it work for anyone else in the long run. My ego got in the way, and I was seeking control over the process instead of focusing on the outcome. I was grateful for the reminder he gave me in the privacy of his truck. Now ten years later, I sat in my chair surrounded by the warmth of the wheelhouse, appreciating my good fortune at having an outstanding crew that I could rely on to get the job done. I looked out at the sea that lay before me where immense, black waves rolled by, their white crests reflected in the great big sodium lights mounted on the mast. Night arrived, and so did the wind.

Attitude is Everything

The boat shook violently as the sea slammed into the bow and broke across the decks. Punching through a twenty-foot wave driven by gale force winds, the Ballad was momentarily blinded by whitewater as the hull lifted itself free of the many tons of icy water.

"Talk to me guys!" I yelled across the intercom to the back deck.

"Yeah, we're fine! We took a big one across the table, and it knocked the anchors off the rack is all. We've just about got 'em lashed together!"

"What about the gear?" I asked.

"Gear's fine! We'll have a few tangled hooks, but it's all lashed down and riding fine!"

At 1:00 a.m., the winds reached past fifty knots and the seas running against the tide were sharp and fierce. Minutes earlier, an enormous wave slammed into the port side, rolling her hard over 50 degrees and sending fountains of water through the scuppers and across the deck. And, it wasn't over yet.

A storm at sea can quickly become a test of sanity as the entire environment becomes a world of shaking, pounding, rising and falling. Simple acts such as standing or walking become chores to be accomplished only through exceptional balance, precise timing and always having something to hang on to. Sleep becomes virtually impossible, and if achieved is sure to be interrupted by the realization that you are now awake, two feet above your bunk and falling fast.

The night became a pattern of thunderous heaves, followed by a sickening lurch as the boat fell into the troughs behind each wave—an exercise in focus while providing an answer to questions of control that many of us, sadly, may never consider or experience.

Wave after wave, after relentless wave, rolled over us. My patience was running low, and my blood pressure was running high. I tried yelling at the ocean, "Stop already! I get the point!" Suddenly, I felt like the people who so often amuse me on the freeway…the ones screaming, yelling and honking their horns while letting other people determine the quality of their day. So I asked myself a question, "What *specifically* do I have control over here? The wind? No, how about the waves? Guess again. So what *do* I have control of?"

I thought back to the earlier days of my fishing career. I remembered how I loved nothing more than a good storm. Ah, the excitement! The danger! I was rough, tough and full of adventure! Now, all that changed. I wanted nothing more than to see the wind stop, and the sea to become calm. I wanted to catch our fish as quickly as possible, in as comfortable a fashion as possible and go home. Suddenly, I knew the answer to my question, "What do I have control over?"

As the *Ballad* pitched and rolled in the darkness, I knew that the only thing I would ever have real control over was, indeed, the most important thing of all… my mind and with it, my attitude. My attitude would determine the ultimate meaning I would attach to any events I experienced and would ultimately be responsible for my future actions and the results I achieved.

"To a worm, digging in the ground is more relaxing than going fishing."

~Clyde Abel~

How, I asked, could two identical events (in this case a storm) energize me at one point in time and then cause incredible stress years later? The difference was in the meaning I gave to those events. When I was younger, my tendency was to focus on all that the storm could provide for me: excitement, adventure and the chance to prove how tough I was. In later years, my tendency was to focus on all that the storm was *taking* from me: peace, security and the ability to finish the job and go home.

I learned this lesson many years earlier, but I suppose sometimes repeat lessons are necessary. When faced with an unpleasant situation, I learned to ask myself the very basic question, "What's good about this?" And sometimes the immediate answer is "Nothing… but if there were, what would it be?" If I ask that simple question enough times and *really* search for an answer, I *always* find something, no matter how small, that will help to change my focus and, consequently, my attitude from that of a victim to the mindset of a winner. In this instance, the weather kept many boats in port and the price high.

Eighteen hours later, I stood at the rail peering down at the ground line gliding up through the cobalt blue depths of the sea. We set and retrieved four five-tub test strings, followed by an additional 75 tubs of gear. The weather was absolutely beautiful with the summer gale of the previous night ending as quickly as it had come, yielding to blue skies and white clouds drifting over the magnificent peaks of the Alaska Peninsula visible on the far off horizon to the north. Our test sets pointed the way to the fish, and we enjoyed tremendous fishing. We were nearing the 40,000-pound mark and with two fresh sets in the water, we would be finished by midnight, setting sail for a high price in Homer with fair winds and a following sea.

CHAPTER FIFTEEN
Who's On Watch

"Have patience with all things but first with yourself.
Never confuse your mistakes with your value as a human being.
You're a perfectly valuable, creative, worthwhile person simply because you
exist. And no amount of triumphs or tribulations can ever change that."

~Saint Francis de Sales~

The Homer Spit is a long, narrow stretch of gravel protruding some seven miles out into the middle of Kachemak Bay. The wide, flat section at the end is covered with an eclectic gathering of tourist shops and charter services surrounding the small boat harbor, home to hundreds of pleasure craft on the north end and commercial fishing boats to the south. The City of Homer built a state-of-the-art unloading dock at the far south end of the boat harbor, and the Ballad lay quietly tied to its pilings, the still waters below reflecting the clouds as they drifted across the sky.

After unloading our catch and cleaning and restocking the boat for our next trip, I gave the crew the night off to relax and enjoy the beautiful evening. Chief and I sat on a large drift log admiring the jagged peaks and glaciers across the bay gleaming in the midnight sun. Our talk, as it did so often, turned to fishing stories as we shared about Highliner seasons and hard lessons from years past.

Hard Work Paid Off

We all have experienced times in our lives when everything seemed to be going our way. We made all the right moves and everything we touched seemed to be turning to gold. Some call it luck; some call it skill; and still others call it destiny. But most often, it comes from the right attitude and plain, old hard work. Whatever the term used, that was exactly what seemed to be happening for me as skipper of the *Ballad*. Everything seemed to be turning to gold while fishing for Dungeness crab near the Trinity Islands off the southwest coast of Kodiak Island during the summer of 1990.

During my second year as Captain of the *Ballad* I paid my dues, learning how to set and haul gear, developing my leadership style (with a parade of crewmen on and off the boat in the process) and figuring out just how and where to find the crab. We started the season off with a bang. With over 800 crab pots to tend, each weighing 80 pounds, we had been fishing aggressively, working non-stop for 36 to 48 hours hauling our pots, re-baiting, setting them back when they were full of crab and stacking the steel and wire mesh cages aboard the boat, moving them to another area if the catch wasn't so good.

My crew consisted of two trusted friends, whom I worked with for several years as a crewman prior to taking over the helm as Captain. Big D and Lane worked well together as we hauled our gear. With fluid motion and a conservation of effort born from experience, they both played an important part in the success we enjoyed so far that summer. We nicknamed our third crewman, "Willie." Don't ask me why, but the name seemed appropriate, and it stuck. A college student, he came to Alaska for the summer like many young men did in the 80's in search of adventure and lots of money. With no prior fishing experience, he was a "greenhorn," but he worked hard, learned fast and seemed to have a good attitude.

Standing Watch

I spent many hours standing watch with Willie teaching him the basics of navigation: how to steer the boat around logs and buoys, plot a course and generally keep the boat on a safe and even course. I would ask him to plot our current position on a marine chart, and then I would sit back and observe the process he went through. Instead of immediately correcting him when he made a mistake, I would ask him questions such as "Are you sure about that?"

or "You might want to check that again, just to make sure."

Of all the crewmen I trained previously, Willie seemed to have a natural talent for navigation, making only a few minor mistakes and usually correcting them himself without my having to suggest he re-check his figures. Only after helping him to find the correct answers would I bring up any mistakes he made, showing him what the consequences of his mistake could have been had he not made the proper correction. Time and again, I would tell him that while he was at the wheel, he was responsible for the lives of three other men. I would have him look out the window at the decking on the bow and put a picture in his mind of the three men sleeping in their bunks just below. "That," I would tell him, "is your most precious cargo. While you're on watch, we're all relying on you to keep us safe." He would nod his head in somber acceptance of the responsibility that was his while on watch.

*"Learning new things won't help the person
who isn't using what he already knows."*

-Anonymous-

The summer was shaping up to one we would not forget. Crabbing was good, the weather even better, and after hauling our gear, we would transit through the treacherous and unmarked channel between Sitkinak and Tugidak Islands, making the eight-hour journey up to Alpine Cove for a few days of R&R. Our days off were spent taking skiff rides on the flat waters protected on three sides by mountains covered with brilliant emerald green foliage that soared up from the waters to over 4,000 feet. We caught king crab and halibut in the cold, clear waters, sport fished for salmon and sat quietly in the tall grass to watch the brown bears fishing in the creeks that poured into the head of the bay. Then, when it was time to fish, we would journey back out to the fishing grounds to begin the cycle once again. At times, I couldn't decide which was more fun…playing on our days off up in the bays or hauling the bounty of crabs aboard from the brilliant, cobalt blue waters. I even developed an off-the-wall theory on where to find crabs, and it seemed to work wonders. If I had a small load of pots rigged for the deeper waters and wasn't sure where to put them, I would scout around to find where the whales were hanging out, and put them there.

California gray and humpback whales end their long northern migration to spend their summer months in the cold waters of the Gulf of Alaska and the Bering Sea, and the area we were fishing in seemed to have no shortage of them. We always seemed to see at least five or six of them in the immediate vicinity, spouting and breaching as they fed upon the same krill and feed that the crabs were dining on. I decided if the whales seemed to congregate in one area, then there must be tremendous amount of feed on the bottom that would not only attract them but the crabs as well. A farfetched theory to be sure that in my later years as a fisherman I realized was somewhat but not entirely ridiculous, but hey…people have achieved greater success on wilder theories than that! Besides, I was on a roll, and everything I touched that summer seemed to be turning to gold. Remember? Yes, this was going to be a summer to be remembered… although for reasons I would have preferred to avoid.

Change of Plans

We had been fishing for a week and a half, and we needed to make the 12-hour run back to the town of Kodiak to unload our catch. As I turned the boat towards town, the sparkles of sunlight reflecting on the ripples created by a light breeze were blinding. The day was brilliantly sunny, perfect for the run to town with not a cloud in the sky and good visibility. The Ballad rode over the low groundswell rolling in from the southeast. I was up for almost 36 hours standing watch for the eight-hour run down from Alpine Cove, followed by a 28-hour stretch at the helm as we ran through our gear one last time. Big D and Lane had also been up the entire time. With the fine weather, the work was relatively easy as far as crab fishing goes with plenty of crabs and few pots to move. The three of us were good friends and enjoyed working together, so we let Willie stay in his bunk asleep while the three of us finished the long shift before turning to the northeast and setting a course for the town of Kodiak.

With Cape Sitkinak 12 miles off our port beam, we were on a straight course over open water for the next ten hours, and my lack of sleep took its toll. My eyelids were heavy, and my head would nod back and forth with the motion of the boat. I was in danger of falling asleep while on watch. To do so would be to commit the ultimate sin on a fishing boat. A man asleep at the wheel leaves the boat unattended, running on autopilot in a straight line without care towards whatever may lie in its path. Hitting a giant, heavy, water-soaked log can cause extensive damage to a boat, let alone the chance of running aground on a submerged reef. More than a few boats met their demise from that very occurrence, and I was determined not to let it happen to the *Ballad*.

"You will always get what you want
if you just help enough other people get what they want."

-Zig Ziglar-

I woke up Willie after his long siesta and called him to stand wheel-watch while I laid down to rest. As I waited for him to get dressed and report to the wheelhouse, my radio, which had been quiet up until now, suddenly crackled to life.

"Calling the *Ballad*, calling the *Ballad*, this is the *Norska*. Do you pick me up Steve?"

"*Norska, Ballad.* Hi, Marko, I pick you up just fine, what's happening?" I replied.

"Yeah, Steve, I've got serious problems with my main engine, and I'd heard you were heading to town and was wondering if you could give me a tow. Where are you right now?"

"Wow, that's no good," I answered. "I'm about 12 miles off Cape Sitkinak right now, but we could probably help you out. Where are you?"

"Well, it sounds like you're kind of on your way then. I'm anchored up in Lazy Bay. I don't suppose you'd want to run all the way in here," said Marko. Lazy Bay was a four and half hour run out of my way, but in the fishing business, there is nobody to look out after you in a situation like Marko faced but yourself and other fishermen, and the time might come when I would need the same type of assistance.

"Hey Marko, no problem. I have changed course, and I am headed your way. Should be there in about four to five hours," I replied.

With that, Willie suddenly appeared at my side ready to stand watch.

"Who was that," he asked.

"The *Norska's* got trouble with their main engine. We're gonna head over to Lazy Bay and give them a tow to town. I will tell you what, we're on course right now for Sitkinak Pass and should be to the pass in about an hour and a half. I'm dead tired and so are Big D and Lane. I want you to stand watch for an hour and a half or until you're two miles from Cape Sitkinak, whichever comes first. Then get me up, and I'll take it through the pass and have Big D and Lane drive up to Lazy Bay after that," I instructed him. I spent another ten minutes with him, having him check our position, determine our course and show me on the chart where I told him to wake me up. Just as I expected, he answered every question without a hitch.

Most boats the *Ballad's* size had a dedicated stateroom in the wheelhouse for the Captain's rest and privacy, but not the *Ballad*. My bunk was against the wall on the port side of the wheelhouse surrounded by windows. While all of that glass provided extraordinary visibility when at the helm, it did not do much for the sleeping side of things with sunshine during the day and reflections from the boats big, high-powered sodium mast lights shining through the windows at night. Still, my crew never complained about my snoring, and the upside was that when I was in my bunk, I was immediately on hand should something go wrong. In addition, if I woke up at night, I could look over and check to see who was taking care of business and who was reading or, God forbid, sleeping. I never experienced any problems with any of my crew in that regard, and as I collapsed into by bunk, I was asleep before my head hit the pillow.

A Fisherman's Worst Nightmare

Suddenly, I was jolted out of my sleep by a tremendous "BOOM" that shook the boat to its core. Looking over to make sure Willie took the boat out of gear to stop the propellers from spinning and save them from damage while the log we must have hit passed under the boat, I was surprised to see he was not there. Almost at the same instant, several more impacts shook the boat in rapid succession. *"BOOM, BOOM, BOOM!"*

Thinking we were in safe water with more than 100 feet of water under the keel, we must be colliding with a group of large logs bobbing together in the water! As I dove for the throttles to pull the engines out of gear, I saw out of the corner of my eye Willie running up the stairs to the wheelhouse. Looking out the windows to see what the problem was, I was shocked to see a small island no more than a quarter mile directly in front of us, not the open ocean, and waves were breaking much closer as the groundswell collided with the reef. My worst nightmare came true. We were aground! With that, the boat slammed into the reef again, the momentum of its 75 tons of weight still carrying us forward at the full speed. Then with a roar followed by a sickening crunch, the Ballad came to a sudden stop, hard aground on the rocks of the submerged reef.

Immediately, I ran across the wheelhouse to sound the General Alarm, but before I took two steps, Lane came barreling up the wheelhouse stairs followed closely by Big D. "What's going on!" they hollered, their eyes ablaze.

"We're aground! Check the engine room and see if we're taking on water! Big D, check the lazarette and the back fish hold! Willie, get the survival suits; put one on and stand by outside the wheelhouse door! Move!" I barked back as the boat was lifted by the next swell only to be slammed back down on the reef with a bone-jarring crash.

With no more than 20 or 30 seconds having elapsed from our initial impact with the reef, Lane and Big D ran down the stairs to check for obvious damage. I spun around and grabbed the microphone to the single-sideband radio. "COMSTA Kodiak! COMSTA Kodiak! COMSTA Kodiak! This is the fishing vessel, Ballad, WTU-7606 over!" I called into the mike. With that, the alarm panels on the dash lit up like a Christmas tree as every high-water alarm on the boat went off. There was no question… the hull had been punctured, and we were taking on water. Once again, the *Ballad* was lifted up by the swell and slammed back down on the reef.

The Coast Guard station in Kodiak is one of the largest in the United States and is home to several patrol ships as well as a fleet of C-130 aircraft and helicopters. The base communications station located on a bluff overlooking Women's Bay just south of town is the nerve center for search and rescue operations and federal law enforcement. The base covers millions of square miles of some of the most treacherous and unforgiving waters in the Northern Hemisphere, including the western Gulf of Alaska and the Bering Sea.

"Fishing vessel, *Ballad*. Fishing vessel, Ballad. This is COMSTA Kodiak, over" came the reply in typical authoritative, yet controlled fashion.

"COMSTA Kodiak, this is the fishing vessel, *Ballad*, whiskey, tango, uniform seven, six, zero, six," I responded, saying our call letters in military fashion so there would be no question as to our identity. "We are aground and taking on water! Our position is five, six, four, zero degrees north, one, five, three, five, niner degrees west over!"

"*BOOM!*" The boat shook as another swell picked it up and sent it crashing down on the reef once more. How much more pounding the *Ballad* could take before she would to break up, I wasn't sure. She was a strong and tough boat, but I could not imagine any boat withstanding the kind of pounding we were enduring and holding together very long. I could feel my body beginning to buzz with adrenaline as a wave of emotions washed over me. I was experiencing fear, anger, frustration, confusion and shame at peak levels of intensity all at the same time.

"The critical ingredient is getting off your butt and doing something.
It's as simple as that."

~Nolan Bushnell~

The funny thing about emergencies is that you never really know how you will react until you are in one. We held regular safety drills, and I spent many hours standing watch, rehearsing in my mind what I would do should a "mayday" situation arise. I would silently mouth a distress call and was always careful to give a position far from the one currently displayed on the GPS so as not to temp fate.

As the boat lifted again to drop back on the rocks, an embarrassing thought flashed through my mind. The single-sideband radio was capable of reaching hundreds of miles, and virtually every boat in Alaska monitored the 4125 MHz frequency I was using to broadcast. Without a doubt, countless fishermen were now aware that the boat I was responsible for was now on the rocks, my crew was endangered, and I was afraid that I must sound like a panicked schoolboy to boot. I was grateful to hear later from a friend who heard my call that I sounded calm, cool and in control. I did not by any means feel that way at the moment, though.

I read the coordinates from the GPS mounted on the ceiling just above the helm to the Coast Guard, but two minutes into our ordeal, I still had no idea where that was. I was too busy trying to keep the boat upright to check the chart, and while I had been asleep, a fog bank crept in, reducing visibility drastically. The only thing I could see, other than the island and breakers in front of us, was the faint outline of land several miles behind us. Although I passed through this general area countless times before, from where we were at the moment, nothing looked familiar.

"Smitty! We've got water in both the lazarette and the back fish hold!" Big D announced as he appeared in the door of the wheelhouse.

"Yeah, I know! We've got water coming in *everywhere*! Lane's down in the engine room trying to pump it out now. Go tell him to see if he can pump the water out of the front fish hold to lighten the boat!" I replied. By pumping the fish hold dry, I was risking losing the load of crab onboard, but I thought that if we could lighten the boat enough, we would have a chance to get free of the rocks. And to be honest, the thought of losing the crab never even entered my mind.

Suddenly, the *Ballad* was lifted again by a swell but higher and more suddenly than before. She heeled over to the starboard side and came crashing down harder than ever. Thrown against the wall, I saw stars as my head collided with the side window with a thud. Then we were lifted once again and heeled over to the port side to slam into the reef again more violently than ever. Things were going from terrible to worse, and they were happening fast.

In It Deep

For a moment, I considered abandoning ship, but one look at the breakers waiting for us if we did quashed the thought immediately. Remember my "most-precious cargo?" Those same men were now working hard to save the boat, and I did not relish the thought of sending them into the frothing whitewater ahead of us. As long as I was Captain of the *Ballad*, I clearly prioritized my responsibilities. Getting my men home safely was number one, followed closely by making sure that the half-million dollar boat I was entrusted with returned in one piece as well. I decided we would not even consider getting off the *Ballad* as long as there was the slightest chance that we could save her. Besides, I reasoned, the boat is not going to sink…we are *already* on the bottom, and she hasn't started to break apart yet.

But, how could we save her? My mind raced for a solution, and an idea formed. I did not know *exactly* where we were, but I could see land several miles behind us. We must have come that way, so it only made sense that deeper water lay that direction. If the boat *was* fatally damaged, and we *were* going to have to abandon ship, then perhaps if we could get to deeper water, we might be able to drift clear of the breakers. Better yet, if the boat stayed afloat long enough, we could run her up on a sandy beach where we could get off safely and perhaps salvage some of the equipment or possibly the boat itself.

Yet just how we would get to deeper water was still a challenge. I knew that when a boat is moving forward, the propellers actually pull water out from under the boat and that if grounded, trying to power your way out of it would actually make the situation worse. That was it! Maybe, just maybe, if we could get most of the water out of the front fish hold and keep from taking on too much additional water from the holes in the hull by putting the boat in reverse, the propellers would actually push *more* water under the boat, helping us even more. I thought if I powered up in reverse when the boat was being lifted on the swell and put it back in neutral just before impact as we were dropped back onto the reef, it might just work. I had no idea whether the propellers were even capable of turning any longer. By this time, as far as I knew, the gigantic, four-foot diameter props were bent and twisted beyond recognition. My idea seemed sound enough, and in the absence of any other options, (other than to let the boat continue to be smashed upon the rocks), I would give it a try.

Adversity introduces a man to himself."

~Steven R. Smith~

"Fishing vessel, *Ballad*. Fishing vessel, *Ballad*. This is COMSTA Kodiak. What is your current status, over?"

"COMSTA, this is the *Ballad*. We're still hard aground and taking quite a beating, but I think we may have a chance to get off. Standby a few minutes while we see what we can do. Over!" I replied.

"Roger, *Ballad*. COMSTA Kodiak standing by."

Then as the next swell lifted the boat, I gingerly put the throttles in reverse and started to power up. The propellers worked! I could feel the vibration as they turned. Then as the boat once again came crashing back down onto the rocks, I quickly put the throttles in neutral. Once again, as the boat lifted, I put the boat in reverse and gently applied power. She was moving! Bit by bit, we moved in reverse perhaps only ten feet or so on each swell, but we *were* moving! Again and again, I repeated the cycle: boat up – power up; boat down – power down.

After almost 15 minutes of this, I started to get discouraged. Would the rocks ever end? How did I know that directly behind was the best route? Then, suddenly as we came down off the last wave, we did not hit quite as hard. The water was getting deeper! After rising and falling with two more swells, the boat came down without impact at last. We were floating! With a surge of victory, I slammed the throttles to full power, determined to get away from those rocks as far and fast as I could. The boat picked up speed. Then without warning, we heard a sickening crash as, under full power, we collided with a reef directly behind us.

"No way!" I shouted. We came so close. I now knew we had a chance, and I was more determined than ever to save the boat. Hopeful determination gave way to faith and a firm belief that as sure as the sun would come up tomorrow, *we were going to get this boat off the rocks*! Then I remembered the initial impact that jolted me out of my sleep. Perhaps the reef we just backed into was part of the one we first hit. We were able to back off one reef. What if we could back over another? I decided to give it a try and began my cycle of power up, power down once again. Slowly, ever so slowly, we began to inch our way over the reef.

Another 20 minutes passed as the *Ballad* pounded on the rocks, but we were making progress. The pumps seemed to be keeping up with the water flooding into the engine room. Repeatedly, we kept trying until once again as we came down off a wave, the impact was not quite as severe. Several more cycles, and we were floating again! With the boat seeming to have survived the collision with the reef behind us while under full power, I was not about to take a chance that it may do so again if another reef was behind us. So, I began to power up gently, the boat moving slowly backwards through the water.

I glanced at the depth meter, and it began to register the depth. The echo on the meter showed the bottom as being less than six feet below the keel, but as we moved backward, slowly but surely, the water began to get deeper: ten feet, then fifteen, then twenty feet. The water was getting deeper! We made it!

I slammed the throttles to full power, backing away as fast as the boat would move. At last, I was sure we put enough distance between us and the rocks to turn the boat around safely without risking another collision and make our way to the relative safety of deeper water...if such a thing existed for a boat full of holes and in danger of sinking.

I called the Coast Guard to give them an update on our situation, and with the rocks of Aiktalik Island behind us, we set course to the northwest through the Sitkinak Straits. My plan was to run for safe harbor in Lazy Bay, a small protected harbor just inside of Alitak Bay, a mere four hours away... if we could only keep the boat afloat that long.

Getting to Safety

As the minutes passed into hours, we determined, barring any further complications, the pumps would be able to keep up with the water flooding into the hull, and we would soon reach the safe waters of Lazy Bay. Another crabber, the *Bold Contender* captained by Don Mathews heard our distress call to the Coast Guard and joined us as an escort. Her presence added tremendously to the growing sense of certainty that we would make it to safety.

During the entire four hours to Lazy Bay, I did not once leave the wheelhouse, and Willie never came upstairs. I was numb with shock and disbelief over what happened. Upon taking command of the *Ballad*, I determined that I would *never* captain a boat that would suffer any major casualties, and yet here I was piloting a boat full of holes with the pumps barely able to keep up with the water rushing in. I took responsibility not only for the lives of my men but for the safekeeping of a boat, a *business* that another man worked incredibly hard to build as well. Now, halfway through my second season, I felt that I utterly failed in my capacity as a Captain.

Upon reaching Lazy Bay, we tied up alongside a salmon tender that was equipped with a deck crane. The *Norska* was tied to the other side of the tender. My crew hurriedly began transferring our catch to the aft hold of Marko's boat while one of his crewmembers and I dove under the *Ballad* to assess the damage.

The primary damage was an enormous 10-foot gash along the underside of the box-keel, and the starboard rudder had been ripped off its mount and bent upwards at a 45-degree angle. We set about stuffing the gash in the keel with raingear, clothing and anything else we could think of to stem the flow of water.

When we did what we could, I caught a ride into shore to use the telephone at the cannery office. I needed to make a telephone call to David— a call that I dreaded.

"You know, by the time you reach my age, you've made plenty of mistakes, and if you've lived your life properly, so you learn. You put things in perspective. You pull your energies together, you change, you go forward."

-Ronald Reagan-

The Responsibility of Leadership

"Hello," I heard David's voice before the first ring completed.

"Hi, David, it's Steve." I answered, downcast. I was not exactly sure how I would explain things to him, but his reply caught me completely off guard.

"John from Eastpoint heard you calling the Coast Guard and gave me a heads up. Is everybody OK?"

"Yeah, everybody's fine, but the boat has a huge tear in the bottom about ten-feet long. I'm sorry, Dave…" I replied, my voice trailing off. I thought for sure my captaining days ended.

"Hey, don't worry about it; those things happen" David replied. "The most important thing is that nobody got hurt. Plus, you got the boat off the rocks. Now we need to focus on how we can get it fixed as quickly as possible so you can get back out fishing. Were you getting' em?"

And with that simple statement, he taught me more about the art of responsibility and leadership than from perhaps any other lesson in my life. Life will always have times where the people we are leading will undergo trials and tribulations, but if we truly believe in them, trust in their ability, and they are willing to learn from their mistakes, then as leaders, we must help them to keep their focus on the desired outcome. David was obviously concerned about the condition of his boat and not happy about what happened, but true to his nature, he was looking for a way to move ahead. He was not a man to spend a lot of time worrying about what "would a', could a', or should a'" happened. He was looking at a much bigger picture than I was capable of seeing at that moment, and it included finishing what started out as a very successful fishing season. The grounding was merely an obstacle (albeit a serious one) to be overcome.

As we talked on the telephone, he helped me to see beyond the moment. We were able to find solutions to the challenges at hand, and soon we created a plan of action. He would call the insurance agency and have them send a marine architect up to Kodiak to survey the boat for damage and recommend repairs. Meanwhile, I would make the boat as seaworthy as possible, and if I felt it was safe to do so, follow along as the *Bold Contender* towed the *Norska* to Kodiak. As I hung up the phone, I was grateful for his understanding, but it did little to lift the weight from my shoulders.

Homeward Bound

The *Dominion* was making barely six knots as she towed the *Ballad* through the same low groundswell that pounded us so mercilessly on the rocks the day before. Mike heard our call to the Coast Guard and immediately set course for Lazy Bay, offering to assist if needed. That he did so turned out to be a blessing. The heavy, cast iron, hydraulic steering quadrant in the lazarrette had been destroyed in the grounding and only by the grace of God it held together long enough for us to reach safe harbor. Now, 24-hours later, we were tethered to the stern of his boat by 250 feet of one-inch cable, straining to free its weight from the water, as it was pulled tight by the surge of the two boats moving through the seas.

The usual 12-hour journey would stretch on into the night with an anticipated landing in Kodiak early the following morning. With the flooding dramatically reduced by the raingear and clothing we had stuffed into the holes in the hull, we didn't need to keep the pumps running continuously. Instead, we were checking the engine room, fish holds and lazarette visually every ten minutes and pumping out when necessary, which seemed to be every half hour.

"Things do not happen; things are made to happen."

~John F. Kennedy~

I had not spoken to Willie, and in the eight hours since our departure from Lazy Bay, he had not set foot in the wheelhouse. We were still in relatively critical condition, but I was feeling more and more confident that the situation was under control. Following my conversation with David and having several uneventful hours since to gather my thoughts, the time came to find out from Willie exactly what led to our grounding, so I went downstairs to find him.

Big D and Lane were at their usual places at the galley table playing another high-stakes game of cribbage. Their eyes followed me as I passed them on the way to the stateroom where Willie lay in his bunk.

"Willie," I said, as he sat up, his eyes glued to the floor. "The insurance company is sending a guy up to Kodiak to take a look at the boat. I want you to write down everything that happened on your watch for him, from beginning to end. I want to know *exactly* what happened while you were on watch. I want to know why you didn't wake me up when I asked. I want to know why you stayed on watch for another two hours past the point where I told you to wake me up, and I want to know how we ended up on those damned rocks. I'm not looking for blame or to point fingers; I just want a statement of facts. Bring it up to me when you have it finished." With that, I turned and went back upstairs to the wheelhouse with Lane following close behind.

"Boy, I thought you were going to let him have it!" he exclaimed, "That was pretty mild. What's up with that?"

"Look, he screwed up big-time," I growled through clenched teeth, the boat surging forward as the towline came tight. "That much is obvious. I know he wasn't at the wheel when we hit 'cause I saw him coming up the stairs when I dove for the throttles. I also know that he didn't even come close to following directions…we were about 15 miles off course, but I want to find out exactly what happened and why. Besides, yelling at him is not going to do any good at this point, and it's not going to get this boat fixed. We've got more important things to worry about than getting mad at Willie."

Conversely, inside I was seething mad. I specifically told Willie to stand watch for an hour and a half and to wake me up at that time or when we were two miles off Cape Sitkinak. He acknowledged my instructions, showed me on the chart where he was to wake me and even pointed out Cape Sitkinak visible through the windows in the distance. Yet, he failed at virtually every aspect of watch keeping. Completely disregarding my instructions, he somehow managed to take the boat far off course and into an area that was clearly marked as dangerous on the chart. Willie had not just made a mistake; he dismissed all responsibility to his "most-valuable cargo." But what angered me the most, as far as Willie was concerned, was that in the 20 hours since we run aground, he failed to offer an explanation or apology. The fact is that everyone makes mistakes, but I had little respect for someone who was unwilling to take responsibility for screwing up after the fact.

> *"Take care of the most important task first. Addressing the tasks that are most important to success first creates a strong foundation upon which to address the less important ones."*
>
> *-Steven R. Smith-*

"I don't know if Big D told you or not," Lane said with a dark look, "but we found a half eaten hot-dog on the table and one in the microwave. That's why he wasn't up here…he was sitting downstairs eating lunch."

So that was it. Not only had he not been in the wheelhouse at the moment of impact, he had not been there much at all. Indeed, several weeks later we would come to find out that while he was waiting for his next hotdog to cook, he fell asleep at the galley table until the moment of grounding. Yet, upon hearing this news from Lane, I wasn't surprised.

"That figures," I answered, shaking my head. "Well, we'll see what he puts in his statement for the insurance guy. It's been a while since we pumped out; you better go check the engine room. Let me know how our patches are holding up." Keeping my anger at bay, I turned to the window to watch the towline ahead, continuing its rise and fall as the swells passed under the boat.

A Highliner Takes Responsibility for His Actions

Twenty minutes, later Lane appeared at my side with fire in his eyes. "Look at this garbage!" he spat out as he threw a piece of paper down on the dash in front of me. In all the years I had known and worked with Lane, I could not ever remember seeing him really mad. He had a can-do attitude coupled with a wonderful ability to see the humor in everything. Not this time.

I reached down, picked up the paper and began to read. As my eyes worked their way down the page, I began to share Lane's anger. Instead of a simple statement of facts as I asked him for, Willie prepared a neatly written piece that read like a 6th grade assignment about his summer vacation. In it, he portrayed himself as an ever-vigilant sailor at the helm keeping an eye out for danger as he stayed his course. He went on to describe an obviously fictitious chain of events that ended with his leaning over to wake me when the boat went hard aground.

"This is a joke!" I snarled as I jumped out of my chair and headed for the stairs. I was incensed. Three steps later, I was down in the galley glaring down at Willie. "What is this crap?! I asked you to write down what happened on your watch, and you give me this?! I saw you coming up the stairs! The radar works fine! You did not wake me up when you were supposed to, and we're 15 miles off course. Don't you get it?!" My voice was getting louder, "I told you I'm not looking for blame...*I just want to know what happened!* Your part ended as soon as we hit the rocks! I am the Captain, and what happens on this boat is *my* responsibility, *no matter what!* It's *my* ass that's in a sling here, and you can't even accept responsibility for your part in it? What a joke!" By now, I was furious. He sank further and further back into the cushions of his seat as I dressed him down. When I finished, I turned abruptly and climbed the stairs back up to the wheelhouse, grumbling as I went.

Another twenty minutes passed and Lane again threw a piece of paper down in front of me, only this time instead of being mad he just looked dumbfounded. I could not believe my eyes as I read Willie's newest composition. Not having succeeded using denial as his tactic for avoiding responsibility, he tried the opposite approach providing a hastily written five-sentence blurb saying it was entirely his fault…he was so tired (after a 28-hour nap)…everything was his fault…blah, blah, blah.

At that point, I lost control. All of the anger and frustration I felt over the last 48-hours came to a head, fueled by his refusal to own up to what he had done. Willie's carelessness put our lives in jeopardy, and as Captain, I was the one who would suffer the consequences should any formal action be taken. As the owner, David would be the one to suffer the consequences financially in shipyard repair costs and increased insurance rates. Moreover as a crew, we *all* would lose money while the boat was laid up, and we were unable to fish. Who was actually at the wheel when we grounded was irrelevant other than as a source of information for the insurance company.

I bolted for the stairs and spent the next ten minutes roaring at Willie. He sat on his bunk, un-moving (a wise thing to do at that particular moment), with his eyes glued to the floor. On a roll, I was barely able to keep from hitting him so hard he would wake up yesterday. Spitting obscenities, I insulted him clear back to his early ancestors.

Finally, my anger was spent. "Willie, when we get to town, you've got three minutes to get off my boat or I'm going to throw your ass and anything you own *overboard*. Got it!?" And with that, I turned and stormed out, leaving him sitting alone on the edge of his bunk as the towline, once again, came tight with a jerk.

"Our lives are the sum total of the choices we have made."

- Dr. Wayne Dyer -

When we finally reached town, I kept my promise to Willie, and as soon as the last tie-up line was fastened to the dock, I had my watch out. He already packed his belongings and made it off the boat and onto the dock in just less than two and a half minutes. He never again worked as a fisherman.

As for the *Ballad*, the damage to the hull was serious but not nearly as extensive as my first wide-eyed look imagined when I scuba dived under her in Lazy Bay. We hauled her out at the shipyard in Kodiak and spent the better part of the next two weeks cutting away the torn box-keel, rebuilding it, fixing the rudder and realigning the propeller shaft. Lane, true to his nature, got quite a bit of entertainment during that time, sneaking up behind me to drop anything large and heavy that was handy so he could watch me jump out of my skin.

Then, as if overcoming a bump in the road (albeit a big one), we put the Ballad back in the water, stocked her full of fuel, bait and groceries and set course, once again, for the crab fishing grounds off of the Trinity Islands. Summer was in full swing, and the crabbing was getting even better. After a strong lesson learned, everything began turning to gold again.

CHAPTER SIXTEEN
Bird Watching

"Not all learning comes from books. You have to live a lot."

~Loretta Lynn~

Two weeks later, the Ballad rolled slowly in the lazy swell as we made our way past the towering escarpments of Castle Cape, a huge, jagged mountain rising from the sea just outside of Chignik Bay. We unloaded just less than 50,000 pounds of halibut in Homer, and we were on our way back to the Aleutians to pick up our final load of the season. If all went well, we would stop in Dutch Harbor, pack the empty spaces left in the fish hold with ice and set sail for the long journey across the North Pacific to unload in Bellingham, Washington. This would be our last trip of the season, and my last as a fisherman. I had a new life awaiting me with Lorraine. We would start a business together, buy a home and settle into life on land…something I had dreamed about for a very long time.

The wheelhouse doors were wide open on this beautiful summer day. We were all enjoying the lazy day as the fresh salt air wafted through the wheelhouse and down through the cabin below. Chief was sitting in the portside chair intently scanning the dog-eared copy of *Powerboat Magazine* in case, I suppose, anything had changed since the last hundred times he leafed through it, dreaming of plying the warm waters of the South Pacific in gleaming 100-foot yachts. Music drifted up from the stereo above the galley where Marty sat writing in his journal. Curtis was in his usual place, lying in his bunk reading a science fiction novel, one of over 50 that he read that summer he would tell me later.

Routines

We worked together for many years aboard the *Ballad*, and we all had our routines o while away the seemingly endless hours as we transited to and from the fishing grounds. After scanning the soaring heights of Castle Cape with the binoculars, I set them back on the dash and settled in my chair. As I gazed out at the calm blue sea ahead of us, a gull flew by my side window and with a fluttering of wings, landed on the very tip of the bow rail above the anchor where he could catch a free ride. I chuckled as I watched him trying to keep his balance on the narrow rail as the boat moved beneath him while at the same time he kept a sharp eye out for a meal. Sea birds are masters of flight, and I have never met a fisherman who didn't enjoy watching them soaring above the waves as they accompanied their boat on its journey.

When standing on the shore looking out to sea, we can easily imagine that we are looking at a vast, empty world of limitless blue windswept waves, but nothing could be further from the truth. Far offshore, away from the sight of land, the waters are indeed ruled by fishes, but the air remains the domain of the birds. Black-footed Albatross soar effortlessly over the waves, carried along with a seven-foot wingspan. Dusky Shearwaters swim with their heads below the surface looking for a meal, and when they spot one, use their wings literally to *fly* underwater in hot pursuit. Storm Petrels, smaller than Robins, flit this way and that searching for even smaller prey. Most abundant of all are the Northern Fulmars.

For the Birds

About the size and shape of a small gull, the usually dark brown Fulmars resemble small fighter planes as they speed along, skimming the tops of the waves on outstretched wings punctuated by an occasional lighting-fast wing beat or two. Suddenly shooting straight up and into a wide, arcing turn, they are the undisputed masters of the air, constantly combing the surface of the sea for a meal, regardless of weather or wind.

The Fulmars are smart, too. Long ago like their cousins the Gulls who live close along the shore, they learned that ships and boats were always a good place to look for food. Soaring around a vessel that is underway, they swoop low across the wake in search of small fish pushed to the surface by the prop-wash. But to the Fulmars, a fishing boat is another story. It is the sea bird's equivalent of winning the lottery—no more working for food (flying, skimming the waves for an occasional squid or minnow). Instead, they get to hang out in the lee, out of the wind and bait and fish guts (i.e.: really good food) are literally dropped in front of them.

"A wise man learns from experience.
A wiser man learns from the experience of others."

-Benjamin Franklin-

When a fishing boat moves slowly through the water retrieving its gear, sorting the catch and baiting their traps and hooks, an abundance of scraps can always be found for the Fulmars. The rich food supply attracts them by the hundreds (and sometimes thousands!) as immense flocks gather around the boat, turning the sea into a mass of squawking brown feathers as they battle amongst each other for food. At night, during the few hours that the fishermen rest (if at all), the flock stays with the boat until morning when the bounty, once again, is available. If the boat moves to a new location, the flock will follow along like a whopping brown cloud, swooping down to jockey for position as soon as the boat comes to a halt.

When fishing for halibut and sablefish, I have spent countless hours watching the Fulmars. With the boat moving slowly through the water or even drifting with the tide, the birds crowd up close to the starboard rail where the ground line was coming aboard. This was a rich place for them to find food, not only from the bait that would fall off any empty hooks that came up, but even more so from the fish heads and entrails thrown overboard by the crewmen cleaning freshly caught fish.

There's One in Every Crowd

Since the very best place to find food was right below the ground line and the scupper where the scraps washed overboard, the birds were constantly fighting amongst themselves for the best position. They reminded me in many ways of people, hurrying back and forth, often in a rush as they tried to outdo each other. First is the Dominant Bird, fearlessly protecting the territory he staked in the best spot, just under the scupper. Second were the Smart Birds, ringing the water right behind them but never really testing the Dominant Bird. "Wanna Be Tough" Birds from farther out would occasionally venture in closer only to be chased away. Even farther out was the General Population. Not wanting to confront the Dominant Bird, they had no hope for a meal until a fish head or other sizable scrap was thrown overboard. Then the whole flock within 100 feet would descend upon it, wings flailing, climbing on top of each other, pecking at anything that moved or got in their way. A mob mentality would take over at times with the birds fighting their way in only to back out when they seemed to forget what they were after in the first place. Farthest out were the rest of the Smart Birds, resting calmly in the water while socializing, preening their wings or sleeping with their wings folded and head tucked in.

Therein lies the mystery. How was it that the Smart Birds were the well-fed ones? Weren't we all taught that the way to the top was to work harder than anyone else? Doesn't nature reward the strongest and toughest as well? Not always. Whether people, birds, or anything else for that matter, the greatest success goes to those who are tough enough to stay in the game but smart enough to play wisely. Work smarter not harder, as the saying goes.

"You can learn a lot by observing."

~ Yogi Berra ~

As I watched, I realized that the Smart Birds would stay just outside the Dominant Birds' territory, only occasionally pushing the boundary. When the Dominant Bird would look their way, the Smart Birds would quickly look the other way and begin casually swimming away, as if their transgression was simply an honest mistake, and they were unaware of what they did.

The Dominant Bird, falling for the ruse would stop any attack he planned. Besides, he was far too busy fighting off the Wanna Be Tough Birds to spend any time squabbling with nice neighbors who never challenged his dominance and only made a "mistake."

Eventually, the Dominant Bird would rush off to the side just as a prime piece of scrap washed out of the scupper, and the Smart Birds would rush in and gobble it up before the Dominant Bird figured out what happened. Eventually, after this happened several times, the Smart Birds would get their fill and fly out to the edge of the flock where they could rest in peace, far away from the maddening rush near the boat. They reminded me of people who stay in the action but work smart and eventually retire to a mountaintop ranch or getaway by the sea.

Meanwhile, the still hungry Dominant Bird would be back defending his territory until eventually a Wanna Be Tough Bird really was, and the Dominant Bird would lose his position, usually to retire out in the General Population. The Smart Birds who retired would be replaced with the next wave of Smart Birds, and the cycle would go on.

At the end of the trip when the boat turned for home and the game was over, anybody who ran around picking on others to prove how tough they were went hungry. Those who were afraid to step into the fray and even try, were left with the scraps that eventually drifted by. Yet, those who were willing to get in the game and used their heads when playing always seemed to get their fill and eventually retired in a nice, peaceful setting on the edge of the crowd where they had room to move, and the neighbors really were nice. Only for the Fulmars, this wasn't a game.

"And neither should it be for any of us," I thought as I slipped out of my chair and down the steps into the galley where Marty nearly finished cooking dinner. "The sea certainly has a lot of lessons for us all."

Donning a set of earmuffs, I opened the door to the engine room and slid down the stairs for a quick check to make sure all was well.

CHAPTER SEVENTEEN
Perseverance IV

"When things go wrong, as they sometimes will;
When the road you're treading seems all up hill.
When the funds are low and the debt seems high,
and you want to smile but have to sigh.
When care is pressing you down a bit,
rest if you must, but don't you quit!

For life is queer with its twists and turns,
as every one of us sometimes learns.
And many a failure turns about,
when he might have won if he'd stuck it out.
Success is just failure turned inside out;
The silver tint of the clouds of doubt.
And you never can tell how close you are;
It may be near when it seems so far.

So stick to the fight when you're hardest hit;
It's when things seem worst that you must not quit!

~Anonymous~

The bright rays of sunshine exploded into a million bright, crystalline flashes as they reflected off the wavelets stirred up by the light breeze that played upon the surface of the cobalt blue waters. The day was beautiful at the Islands of Four Mountains. The perfectly symmetrical cinder cones of active volcanoes giving this area its name burst forth from the surrounding waters, up through bands of green tundra covering their flanks before giving way to steep slopes of shale and ending their journey skyward in sharp, snow covered peaks surrounded by rings of puffy gray and white clouds.

Although our five-day journey from Homer took us nearly 200 miles west of Dutch Harbor to the Islands of Four Mountains, the primary port for the Bering Sea fisheries, we traveled barely a quarter of the length of the long, unbroken chain of islands that made up the Aleutians.

The Aleutian Islands stretch nearly 1,500 miles westward from Unimak Island in the east to Attu Island at their westernmost tip and act as lonely sentinels guarding the boundary between the southern reaches of the Bering Sea and the vast reaches of the North Pacific Ocean. In this wild, desolate and untamed place of uncommon beauty, many of the storms that pound the northern waters of Alaska are born. The weather is unpredictable, and the tidal currents treacherous as the cold waters of the Bering Sea are drawn through the relatively narrow passes between the many islands out into the North Pacific and back again as the cycle completes.

"I think I see a marker flag over there, about a quarter mile out at ten o-clock off the port bow," Curtis said, "Is there somebody else fishing in this area?"

"No…I can't see anybody on the radar," I replied, turning the range on the daylight display to twenty miles. "As far as I know, we're the only ones here, and we're almost three miles from where we set our gear. Maybe a lost set's still in the water from the last boat that fished here."

The *Ballad* rolled slowly to starboard in the calm seas as I changed course to steam in the direction that Curtis reported seeing a flag. He seemed gifted with incredible eyesight and after many years of fishing with him, experience taught me that when he said he saw something out on the sea, something was probably out there worth investigating. As the boat settled on the new course, I dialed into the autopilot, picked up the heavy, black, rubber-coated binoculars from the dash in front of me, raised them to my eyes and began scouring the flat, distant waters for the telltale flash of an orange pennant affixed to the top of one of the tall, 10-foot poles that longline fishermen routinely used to mark the location of their gear.

"Yeah, I see a flag out there. It looks like one of ours too..." I said to no one in particular. Putting the binoculars down, I rechecked our position and crosschecked that with the coordinates from my logbook where I wrote down the locations of our sets. Sure enough, we were just less than three miles from the nearest string of gear that we set just one hour earlier. "Well, maybe it came untied or something. You sure you guys got the knots tied good and tight?" I asked, already knowing the answer.

"Yeah, Chief and I tied all the knots. We got 'em tight and didn't have any problems setting the gear," Curtis replied. "It must've broken off or something."

"That's not a good sign," I said, understating the obvious.

Longline sets typically consist of ¼-½" diameter nylon "ground line" with a series of short lengths of twine tied at intervals of 3-8 feet holding the baited hooks. Stretched along the rocks and ridges of the sea floor for up to three miles, the longline set is marked only by a set of buoys and flagpole that are, in turn, tied to the anchors placed at each end of the set to hold it in place. Fishing in waters that can exceed a half-mile in depth, a broken buoy or ground line can quickly result in lost gear. We had a set of heavy steel grapple hooks onboard that we could use to drag along the ocean floor in hopes of snagging any lost gear, but the deep waters we were fishing and the strong tides of the Aleutians made it akin to searching for a proverbial "needle in a haystack." Any gear lost where we were was likely to remain lost forever.

As the boat pulled up alongside the out-of-place set, Curtis reached out with a long bamboo pole, deftly hooked the line between the buoys and the flagpole and pulled them aboard. As the power block used to haul the line aboard began its long, soft, monotonous growl, I settled back in my chair and looked out on the wide expanse of Open Ocean that lay unbroken before me for a thousand miles before lapping up against the cold, distant shores of far-off Siberia. My thoughts began to wander as memories of seasons past spent fishing these waters for King crab, halibut and black cod flooded my mind.

Drifting Gear

Jolted from my reverie by a harsh, metallic banging against the side of the boat, I walked out onto the deck overlooking the hauling station at the starboard rail where Curtis was standing. Yelling out "Anchor!" he manhandled the 80 pounds of rusted steel over the side of the boat, quickly untied it and began hauling the ground line aboard. Having thought we would be hauling nothing more than a broken buoy line, I was surprised and somewhat concerned to see the anchor come aboard followed by a substantial amount of ground line still in the water. We set the gear during the period of calm water between the flood and ebb tides and no substantial current had been tugging at the buoys when we pulled them aboard, so what could have caused this part of the set to beak away and drift so far so fast?

Twenty minutes later, we retrieved 18 of the original 20 tubs of gear from the set, but the anchor and buoys from the second end were nowhere in sight. As soon as the gear was safely aboard the boat, I put the *Ballad* in gear and set a course for where we dropped the other end, in hopes of retrieving the missing buoys, flag and anchor. We went less than two miles before I spotted another one of our flags. Checking our position, we confirmed that it, too, was out of place!

"Got another one to pick up, guys," I announced over the loudspeaker as I changed course toward the flag. As with the set we just pulled, the buoy line was slack and the flagpole and buoys floated high and clear in the water, indicating little or no current. What was going on here? My mind whirled with thoughts of submarines snagging on buoy lines and dragging our gear hither and yon. "Submarines!" I thought, "Yeah right, or maybe a giant whale that's getting a good laugh at our expense!" In spite of ridiculous scenarios such as these were, that is all that would come to mind.

"Persistence in a flawed plan is folly."

~Steven R. Smith~

The morning soon evolved into an afternoon of frustration. The weather was beautiful and the nearby islands gleamed in the sunshine flooding down from a cloudless, blue sky. With no winds at all, the slick surface of the sea shone like a mirror, while in the shadow of the *Ballad* the crystal, clear waters yielded a view into the depths where we could see the fish struggling on the ground line a hundred feet down as we pulled it towards the surface. The perfect fishing weather we had been blessed with was a treat compared to the usual fog banks, rain and wind that seemed all too common in the Aleutian Islands during the summer months. But, our enjoyment was tempered by the discovery that all of the gear we set that morning moved. Instead of running to the coordinates that marked where our end markers should be, our strategy soon became one that consisted of hours of criss-crossing the calm seas, scouring the horizon in all directions looking for flags and buoys followed by 30 minutes to an hour of hauling gear when one was found. Inevitably, every set we found was broken somewhere along its length and the resulting movement of the gear along the bottom yielded a catch far below what I expected in this area.

Our ability to search for the scattered gear was soon brought to a halt by the coming darkness. That morning we placed five sets of gear using ten anchors and end markers, one for each end. Although we retrieved most of the ground line we set, by nightfall we only retrieved five of the ten anchors and end markers, and the likelihood of finding them the following morning after another tidal cycle was remote. I decided to call for some advice.

Always be Flexible

Powering up the giant single-sideband radio, I made a ship to shore call to Don Jester, the owner and Captain of the Sea Valley II, and one of the best Longline fishermen in the fleet. He fished these waters extensively, and I thought if anyone could shed some light on the mystery I was facing, he could. "Hey, Grandpa. Ya picking me up OK?" I asked, using the nickname David gave him years ago.

"Yeah, Smitty, I get you just fine. What's up?" he asked.

"Well, I'm kind of stumped. I'm at the Islands of Four Mountains, and I set five sets of gear this morning. For some reason the ground line broke on every one of them, and they drifted miles from where I set 'em. I got most of the ground line back but only got back one end marker and anchor per set." I explained, "Any suggestions?"

"Sure, the tide can be really strong at that spot during the flood, so make sure you're careful what time you set your gear." he answered.

"Well, I've checked and re-checked the tide book, and we set all of the gear during the slack water before the ebb tide, but all the sets moved anyway. We've spent the whole afternoon running all over the place looking for flags and buoys trying to get the gear back."

"That could be part of the problem," came his reply crackling over the long-range radio transmission. "We never used flags when we fished there. The flagpole causes too much drag when the tide flows, and it'll suck the buoys down where the water pressure will pop them. Are you catching any fish on the gear you're getting back?"

We talked for several more minutes before signing off. I hadn't thought of the drag in the water caused by the flagpoles, and although the tides did not seem to flow all that hard, I knew that appearances could be deceiving. We would set again in the morning, keeping the flagpoles onboard and using buoys alone to mark the ends of our sets. Seeing no boats on the radar screen, I re-checked our position, making sure we were a safe distance from shore before shutting down the main engines. We would drift through the night on calm waters that sparkled in the darkness with the brilliant reflections of a billion stars overhead.

When It Rains, It Pours

"You've gotta be kidding me!" I shouted at the flat, blue ocean that lay before us. The day was fast becoming an instant replay of the day before. Even after making the sets without flagpoles, our gear still became hopelessly scattered, and we spent yet another day searching for missing end-markers in near perfect weather. As darkness once again began to fall, I sat in my chair glaring out the window, my mind whirling as I searched for an answer to the challenges we were facing. We started the trip with 12 anchors, 24 buoys and 14 flagpoles to mark the ends of our longline sets. After two days of chasing scattered gear under sunny skies, we retrieved most of the ground line from our sets, catching just over 18,000 pounds of halibut in the process, but the missing end markers left us just 4 anchors, 6 buoys and 9 flagpoles…enough to make only two sets.

"At this very moment, you are WHO you are and WHERE you are because of what you've allowed to inhabit your goal-box."

~Richard Gaylord Briley~

The possibility of filling the boat and making the four-day run to Homer to sell our fish on the fresh market for a higher price were fading fast, but I was not ready to give up quite yet. Determined to find an answer, I picked up the tide book and began once again thumbing through its well-worn pages. Somehow our gear was being pulled out of place, and I was sure the answer lay somewhere in the book before me. We set during the slack water before the ebb tide and when the water did begin to flow, it seemed to be very mild at best.

Fishing the tides can be tricky, and the area around the Islands of Four Mountains that we were fishing in was no different. With a strong flood tide capable of carrying our gear far from where it had been set as it drifted down through the depths before settling on the ocean bottom, I was careful to set our gear during the period of calm water just before the beginning of the ebb tide. Experience taught me that the ebb tide in this area was relatively benign and should pose no problems for us. My plan was to set and haul our gear during these times, spending the duration of the stronger flood tide untangling the mass of gear that had been brought aboard and re-baiting it in readiness for the next day's set.

In Plain Sight

I stared hard at the page containing the tidal predictions I checked and re-checked so many times in the past two days as if through sheer willpower I could force the book to reveal its secret. And that is just what happened. Only instead of a miraculous revelation presenting itself accompanied by the grand sound of heavenly trumpets, the answer just lay on the page in cold, black letters, wide open and obvious for all to see. I must have looked at that page fifty times in the last two days to check the exact time that the tides would change, but I never checked the volume of tidal flow right next to it.

The volume of tidal current is simply a measurement of the amount of water that is being moved by the gravitational pull of both the Sun and the Moon as the ocean waters are pulled towards the equator. When the Sun and the Moon are opposing each other, these gravitational forces work against each other, and the tidal flow is minimized. When they are in alignment, their forces combine and tidal flow is much greater. With the Aleutian Islands creating a barrier between the cold waters of the Bering Sea to the north and the limitless expanse of the Pacific Ocean to the south, the tidal flow can reach mammoth proportions as the northern waters are pulled through the narrow passes between the islands before changing direction and flowing northward once again.

While the fine weather and calm waters helped to disguise the tidal currents on the surface, it was now apparent that in the depths below lay a raging torrent of water forcing its way through the pass to the south before changing direction to flow northward again with each change of the tide. We were fishing during the largest tides of the year, and the force of the water was literally dragging our gear across the jagged rocks that lay on the ocean floor 900 feet below. I did not do my homework and not checking the tide table more closely before leaving Homer, a thousand miles to the east, I made a major mistake. Had I done so, we likely would have stopped in Kodiak for some R&R.

"In times like these, it helps to recall that there have always been times like these."

– Paul Harvey –

Picking up the radio, I put in a ship-to-shore call to David. I informed him of the situation with the tides and that I did not see any way we would be able to load the boat in time to make the run to Homer to sell the fish on the fresh market. I suggested we sell the fish we had in Dutch Harbor, wait for a week and try again when the tides begun to diminish.

"No, you don't need to do that!" he answered. "Just go inside and fish by the islands where there's less current. Lot's of guys have caught fish in there. You've got another couple of days of leeway to get your load."

"I know I've got a couple of days, but I've fished in there, too, and have never found anything in the shallows, at least not at this time of year," I replied, repeating my earlier concerns. "Besides, right now I've only got 12,000 pounds of fish onboard. I'd rather sell what we've got in Dutch and save the bulk of our quota to catch when the tides subside, and we can deliver it in Homer for a better price."

"Aw, just go in and fish by the islands. You're bound to come up with something!" I could tell by his answer that David was becoming a bit irritated with me. His style was "Damn the torpedoes, full speed ahead!" and my reluctance to fish during the high tides was not playing very well.

"Yeah, OK, I'll try the shallows in by the islands. Talk to you later. *Ballad* clear," I said hanging up the microphone in frustration. I felt as if I was between a rock and a hard place. I had always been willing to put in the extra hours, go the extra mile and make a situation work, regardless of what it took. I also understood the difference between trying to smash through an obstacle as opposed to going around it, and in my view, continuing to fish was simply smashing up against an obstacle. Oh well, I had a bit more time left and maybe we would get lucky…

Perseverance and a Faulty Plan

The next morning, we awoke once again to beautiful blue skies and a calm sea. We considered it a treat when the opportunity arose to fish in the shallows that lay at the bottom of the island cliffs that soared up from the waters. With only four anchors left, we made our two sets less than an eighth of a mile from the base of the cliffs, and the location was spectacular. Multitudes of birds soared overhead on the currents of air that were sweeping up the face of the dark rocks rising nearly straight up for several hundred feet before yielding to an explosion of yellow and white wildflowers covering the tundra on the flanks of the mountain. At the base of the cliff where we set our gear, the water was flat, calm and crystal clear. We imagined that in the rays of the sun we could see nearly to the rocky bottom hidden by seaweed 50 feet below.

Fishing so close to the islands could be an exciting venture during late July and August when the halibut migrated into the shallows to feed. The fish caught were often huge, weighing in excess of 100 pounds and still wild with fight after their short ride up from the bottom. As the mid-June sun shone down on the waters surrounding the Islands of Four Mountains, chances were slim that we would enjoy such fishing. But, the beauty of the place made the day enjoyable, nonetheless, as we spent several hours drifting in and out of the shadows of the cliffs listening to music and enjoying the sunshine while giving our gear an opportunity to catch fish.

Hauling back our first set, my suspicions were confirmed. We probably would have been better served if we just spent the day lazing in the sun without setting any gear in the water. We caught less than 500 pounds of fish, and one of the anchors became snagged on the rocky bottom below. Despite 45 minutes of maneuvering the boat this way and that in an attempt to pull it free, the ground line finally snapped, and the anchor was lost. After the second set, the whole situation became somewhat of a cruel joke. We spent 30 minutes hauling gear and another hour spinning the boat in circles, throwing out extra line and then reeling it back in again in an attempt to pull the anchors free.

By early afternoon, our efforts were rewarded with less than 1,000 pounds of fish caught and all but one of our anchors lost. So much for catching fish in the shallows…with no way to hold our gear on the bottom, we were effectively out of business.

Catching a Creative Idea

As we slowly motored out away from the island, I had to laugh at the situation in which we found ourselves. We went fishing during the worst possible time of year, caught relatively few fish and lost a good portion of our gear in the process. All the same, we persevered! Hah! While perseverance is often the difference between success and failure, doing the same thing over and over again and expecting a different result is just another definition of insanity. We tried a number of different approaches, but the bottom line was we had not been able to overcome the obstacle of the tides.

A part of me was still determined not to give up, nevertheless, and as I put the boat on a course that would take us just north of Unalaska Island on our way to Dutch Harbor to unload, an idea began to form in my mind. A gully lay on the ocean bottom about 10 miles ahead of us where we tried several times to drop our gear. I knew that if we could get our gear to land between the two ridges that formed the edges of the gully, we would find fish there - lots of fish! Perhaps with a bit of luck, we could catch our quota after all. But with only one anchor left, how could we get our gear to sink to the bottom? No sooner had I asked the question than I remembered the big marine battery parked on the deck.

The *Ballad* carried two great big marine batteries in the wheelhouse to provide power for much of the electronic navigation systems and radios. One of the large 100-pound batteries failed just before we left Homer. It was replaced with a new one and was now tied securely just outside the galley door until it could be disposed of at our next port of call. I walked out onto the back deck and stood there looking at the two-foot long, black plastic battery. It was at least as heavy as our biggest anchors had been, and with its relatively compact size, it just might be able to sit on the bottom in such a way that it could hold the ground line secure for one quick set.

"Hey, Curt," I called, "Do you suppose this battery's heavy enough to work as an anchor if we were to make one more set?"

Curtis walked over and stood beside me looking at the battery. "Yeah, I suppose so. Why? Are you planning on making another set?" he asked, looking at me doubtfully.

"Yeah, I was thinking about it," I replied. "You know that gully we were trying to get our gear in? I know fish are in there, and if we can get a set to land in the right spot, maybe we'll get lucky. What'cha think?"

He chuckled at the ridiculousness of the whole situation. Curtis had been a longline fisherman for as long as I had, and we fished together as crewmembers for years before I took command of the *Ballad*. I respected his opinion and given the long shot I was proposing, if he thought it was a dumb idea, I wouldn't do it. "Sure, why not!" he smiled, his eyes sparkling with good humor. "We can't do much worse than we did this morning!"

"OK," I nodded, "Let's give it one more shot. Get ready to make a set with 1,200 feet of buoy line on both ends. I know the fish are there! We just need to land the gear in the right place." And with that, we set out what became known as "The Battery Set."

We set out 25 tubs of ground line stretching for just over a mile. With another hour before the end of the ebb tide, I set our gear nearly a mile up current from where I wanted it to land in hopes that it would drift downstream into the gully as it sank. My plan was a long shot at best, but luck was with us, and it worked! Perhaps now we would catch some fish!

I knew that the tides were against us, and I knew that with only one set in the water we would be lucky to fill our quota, but I also knew in my gut, fish were in that gully, and I learned to trust my instincts in that regard. Although we encountered problems with drifting gear and broken buoy lines during the past several days, giving me little evidence that we would find fish in the gully, whenever I felt such certainty in the past, I had rarely been wrong. And with our gear finally landing in the right place, I felt confident we would catch fish. Even if we only caught half of what we needed to fill our quota, perhaps we could do the same thing the next day and finish our trip anyway.

I still didn't trust the tides, though, and decided to drift right alongside the buoys that marked the first end of our set. Double-checking the tide tables, I figured we could let the gear soak for nearly two hours before the current would change direction again. If the buoys showed any sign whatsoever that the current was changing, my crew was standing by, ready to start hauling immediately. We were not going to let this set get away!

"Consistent action is the key to success. But if that action is not effective and based on realistic expectations, the door will remain closed."

~Steven R. Smith~

We let the gear soak for two hours, and the buoys had not drifted at all. The waters seemed calm and my confidence grew with each passing minute. The moment of truth was fast approaching when we would discover whether my hunch paid off. Unfortunately at times, the best-laid plans of men are doomed to failure, and as I reached for the loudspeaker microphone, my hand froze in mid-air as I stared out the window in disbelief at the sight of the tall, jet-black dorsal fins of Orcas suddenly cutting through the waters surrounding our buoys!

A Whale of a Challenge

The abundant pods of Orcas or Killer Whales that inhabited the Aleutian Islands had long ago developed a taste for the black cod that fishermen pulled from the depths along the island chain. Since black cod live beyond the normal diving depths of the Orca, the sleek black and white whales learned that when a Longliner was hauling its gear from the depths, the struggling fish on hooks presented an easy and tasty meal. They would dive down below the boat, at times even holding their position less than 10 feet below the surface of the water, to pluck the helpless fish brought up from the depths.

Intelligent animals and blessed with amazing swimming speeds, the Orcas would roam the islands in search of their natural foods, but they learned that the whine of hydraulic motors and idling diesel engines echoing through the sea indicated a Longliner was working, and that meant an easy meal. They would race to the unfortunate fishing boat to begin their feast, literally stripping the ground line clean, leaving nothing for the fishermen but a collection of bent hooks and broken gangions. When the whales showed up, a fisherman had no choice but to leave the area. In the past, they had not been much of a concern for fishermen seeking halibut in the relatively shallower waters. Yet in the past several years, I heard more and more instances where they developed a taste for halibut as well, and today they came to eat ours.

The next 30 minutes presented a comical effort as we attempted to drive them away by yelling at them and pounding on the sides of the boat as I first tried to chase them and then lead them away from our gear. A hopeless strategy, the whales simply swam circles around the boat while waiting for us to begin hauling. If whales can laugh, I would imagine we provided quite the entertainment for them as the boat circled this way and that. We moved several hundred yards from our buoys in our maneuvering, and as I looked back for the buoys, I realized our time was up. The current changed, and the buoys were now creating a wake as the tide surged around them.

"We gotta start hauling now guys!" I yelled into the loudhailer. With the sudden change in current and the speed with which it was beginning to flow, my concern changed from the whales eating our catch to just getting our gear back.

Pulling up to the buoys, all four crewmen strained heavily against the buoy line until they had enough slack to put it into the hauler. I hurriedly ran downstairs, put on my raingear and went to the hauling station. The engines growled, and the buoy line strained against the surge of current as we hauled the anchor from the bottom. Once we had the anchor up, we would be hauling with the current. And if we hauled fast, we would be able to get our all of our gear back. As the line came tight yet another time, suddenly we heard a loud "Snap!", and it was gone. The buoy line broke!

Without bothering to remove my raingear, I sprinted up to the wheelhouse and spun the boat around. The large twin diesels roared as I pushed them to their limits, literally racing the tide to the other end of our set. I could see the rip current in the water where the ending ebb tide flowing to the south was colliding with the flood tide flowing to the north as the tide changed. If we made it to the other end, we might have a chance at getting most, if not all, of our gear back before the current reached its peak.

"Just Do It!"

~Nike®~

Reaching the last end of our set, I spun the boat around, and Curtis whipped the buoys aboard and started hauling the gear aboard. Running downstairs, I jumped to the rail and slammed the hauler controls to their limit. What little luck we had was still on our side, and three minutes later, up came the battery. I heaved it aboard and stood at the rail with a gaff hook in my hand that I would use to pull any fish aboard. The whales had yet to appear.

Suddenly I saw a flash of white in the water, and I thrust my gaff hook down and brought a beautiful 40-pound halibut aboard. Then another...and another. A fish was on nearly every hook! My hunch paid off!

Again and again, I pulled fish aboard, and the catch bin started to fill up. Then as suddenly as it begun, nothing. We hauled for another five minutes without seeing a single fish. I looked up to see a dorsal fin cutting through the water 30 feet away as an Orca dove down for another meal. My hunch paid off; the fish were indeed in the gully, and we beat the tide to the other end. But now the whales were eating virtually every fish that we hauled from the depths. Looking over at my crew, our eyes met. We all began to laugh. The situation was too ridiculous to be mad.

In the end, we would haul nearly all of our ground line back and set course for Dutch Harbor. We offloaded 20,000 pounds of hard-earned halibut for a price that was nearly 50 cents less per pound than we would have been paid in Homer. Deciding to take two weeks off until the tides settled down, we tied the boat to the dock and boarded a flight to Anchorage. I reflected back on all that went wrong with the trip. My failure to check the tides before leaving Homer doomed our trip from the start. A harsh lesson was learned, and I would not make the same mistake again. I picked up my logbook and wrote "THIS SUCKS!" in big, bold letters across the page. As I looked down at what I wrote, I considered another point of view. While we weren't close to achieving what we set out to do, the weather was beautiful; we enjoyed an adventure together, and our ingenuity in using the battery as an anchor would make a good story. After all, when things do not work out as we have planned, if we look hard enough, we will always find something that holds a value that cannot be measured by money.

And with that, I got ready to meet Lorraine at the airport. She was coming to visit during our break. In just seconds of seeing her, my frustrations would disappear and were replaced with appreciation.

CHAPTER EIGHTEEN
Thoughts are Things

"Believe that you will succeed.
Believe it firmly, and you will then do what is necessary
to bring success about."

~Dale Carnegie~

"Hey, Curtis! Put in another tape will ya? This one's been playing for four hours straight!" Marty hollered over the heavy metal noise blaring from the cheap plywood speaker boxes that were tied to the tub racks on the port side of the shelter deck.

"What! What! I can't hear you!" Curt yelled back with a mischievous smile as he ducked under the overhang and disappeared into the galley. Moments later the raucous noise we endured for the last several hours mercifully came to a halt. Looking up from watching the blur of Chief's hands as he baited the tub of hooks, I could see the huge snow covered peaks in the distance presenting a sharp contrast to the expanse of dark blue water that seemed to race by as the Ballad cut through the choppy seas at 10 knots. We were on our way back out to the Island of Four Mountains after unloading just about 20,000 pounds of halibut and picking up a fresh compliment of shiny new anchors and flags. With the diminishing tides and the beautiful weather, we could see the light at the end of the tunnel of a long season. One more run to

Homer followed by another trip to the Four Mountains followed by the long trip across the North Pacific, and we would be nearly finished.

Suddenly, a slightly different flavor of distorted, heavy metal noise started blaring forth from the vastly overpowered speakers. My ears hurt. I couldn't understand how these guys could stand out on deck and subject their ears to such abuse. Don't get me wrong, I enjoy music as much as the next guy, but without any bass to balance out the scratchy, screaming treble, well, that was just too much for my ears. Grabbing a bagful of gangions that needing tying, I skipped across the deck as a flood of water swept across the deck boards and up the stairs to the wheelhouse narrowly escaping with dry feet.

As I sat in my chair tying gangions, I thought back to other boats and crews in years past and how different the conversations were aboard those that were consistently successful and those that were not. As I sat reflecting, my mind drifted back to a trip 12 years earlier. An ill-fated trip aboard the *Cape Spencer* stood out in my mind as a classic example of the mindset aboard some of the boats in the fleet.

Falling Short

Rolling broadside in the sharp eight-foot seas, the cold sea-spray was kicked up across the deck of the 48-foot *Cape Spencer* as she made her way to the halibut grounds off the southern tip of Kodiak Island. I remembered walking over to Chris as he stood at the table in the middle of the deck methodically baiting the thousand hooks we would set in the upcoming days.

"Hey, Buddy," he called out over the wind as I approached, "What's happening?"

"Oh, same old same old I guess," I answered, picking up a knife and cutting a long frozen piece of octopus into bait-sized chunks. "Looks like the winds kicking up a bit. I sure hope it doesn't blow too hard for the opener."

"Yeah, no kidding. Wouldn't that be our luck, getting blown off the fishing grounds…" Chris replied as he poked one of the steel hooks through another piece of bait.

"Well, Paul told me earlier that the weather forecast was calling for southeast winds increasing to 25 knots. Hopefully if it does blow, we'll be protected somewhat by the southern tip of the island, but if it shifts to the south at all, it's gonna get pretty rough," I answered back.

"Hope in one hand and spit in the other.
Then see which one fills up first."

~ Bill Gouldd ~

Although the time was nearly eleven-thirty in the evening, the "midnight sun" that bathed the northern latitudes during the summer months was able to break through the low-hanging clouds in places. Steep mountains rose above black cliffs bordering the southeast coast of Kodiak Island, and now brilliant green tundra shone through in sun lit patches, supporting Kodiak Island's nickname as "the Emerald Isle." Protected from the wind and sea spray by thick, heavy raingear, we continued to share the usual crewmen's banter as we baited hook after hook.

Carrying a crew of four plus a Captain, we planned to fish the halibut opener and then re-rig the boat and set course for the 20-hour voyage across the Open Ocean to Prince William Sound. We would then spend the summer fishing the immense schools of salmon making their final journeys to the myriad of streams that poured into the sound. As Chris and I stood at the table baiting hooks, we daydreamed about striking it rich, first on the halibut grounds and then upon the quiet waters surrounding the countless islands topped with towering fir trees that dotted the sound.

"Could you imagine if we landed on 'em big time during this opener?" he asked, his eyes sparkling with the thought of filling the boat with the gigantic, white-sided halibut.

"No kidding! I heard the price would be around a buck a pound before we left. I dunno how much this boat'll hold, but I'll bet we could get 40,000 pounds on her if we're lucky," I replied with enthusiasm.

Chris laid down the file he was using to sharpen a hook that became dull with rust and looked out at wind-chopped waters. "Yeah, I sure hope we do well…I sure could use the money. I spent everything I had skiing this winter, and I'm just about down to my last dollar. How'd your king crab season go?" he asked as he picked up another piece of bait, poked the hook through and hung it on the rack beside him.

"Oh, we did OK. Average I guess....I couldn't believe it though…ya know the Courageous? They were fishing just outside of us the whole season, and they put in over 100,000 pounds! We were *that* close! Can you imagine? The crew probably made over fifteen grand in a week and a half!" I answered.

"Whoa, really? Man I wish we could get lucky like that sometime…" Chris's voice drifted off into the wind as we continued our chores, sharing dreams of success, and wishing that they might someday come true. Just then, the clouds began to glow in the soft pastel hues brought on by the gathering twilight.

The Right Stuff

Back on the Ballad I gathered up a handful of freshly tied gangions as I thought about how that trip aboard the *Cape Spencer* turned out like so many others: a partially full fish hold and dreams of success once again put on the back burner. I tied the gangions in a bundle and threw them onto the pile of finished gangions on the floor in the corner, and I shook my head in amusement, a small smile playing across my face as I heard yet another flavor of heavy metal beginning to blare out of the poor speakers out on deck. My, how things had changed.

I thought of the countless "B.S." sessions that took place aboard the *Ballad* or any other boat that was a consistent producer. With an easy sense of confidence, the crew told fishing stories from years past, talked about families and friends, and when the subject of the present trip *did* come up, the success of the trip was always considered a forgone conclusion. Instead of hoping and wishing for a good trip, the crew would spend their time talking about how they were going to spend the money that they knew they were going to make.

> *"Faith is the absence of doubt,*
> *the ability to know without question that something is true."*
>
> *~Steven R. Smith~*

"Man, when this seasons over, I'm going' to Hawaii!"

"Yeah? Well I'm gonna buy a brand new Harley-Davidson motorcycle and ride it down the California Coast! What're you gonna do?"

"Me? My wife and I are building a new house, and we're going to put in a new patio!"

"Hey! What's for dinner! And somebody change that friggin' tape will ya? It's been playing for nonstop for two days!"

And so it was on the *Ballad* under the watchful gaze of the Four Mountains. The tides slacked off, and the fish were right where we found them on the previous trip with what become known as "The Battery Set." After two easy days of fishing, we steamed back toward Homer with a fish hold stuffed full of clean, white-sided halibut on their way to the fresh market. The sea remained like a millpond, its flat and glassy surface undisturbed by even a puff of wind. Nearly finished with our season, our spirits were high. We were that much closer to the trip to Hawaii, the motorcycle ride down the coast, the new patio or whatever else came to mind in the next several weeks. And, I was one-step closer to retirement as a commercial fisherman and my new bride.

CHAPTER NINETEEN
Deliverance II

"You of little faith, why are you so afraid?"
Then he got up and rebuked the winds and the waves,
and it was completely calm."

~Matthew 8:26, NIV~

Early September found the Ballad steaming the waterways between the numerous small islands off the southern coast of the Alaska Peninsula. Winding its way past the villages of Sand Point, King Cove, and the aptly named Cold Bay, the "Inside Passage" with its relatively protected waters was the primary transit route from the Gulf of Alaska to the Bering Sea. It was also the shortest due to the countless reefs that dotted the outside waters up to 50 miles offshore.

After delivering our last load in Homer, we were on our way back out to Dutch Harbor to check in. Then we would travel another 200 miles along the Aleutian chain, past Unalaska and Umnak Islands to the fishing grounds off the Islands of Four Mountains that we left just a week and a half earlier. As we traveled west, the landscape began to take on a "wilder" look as the trees and forests that dotted the coast near Kodiak slowly gave way to the barren, wind swept tundra, characteristic of southwest Alaska.

We passed Sand Point early that morning and as the sun brought on the day, I tuned in to listen to Peggy Dyson's morning weather forecast. Peggy had been broadcasting the National Weather Service marine forecasts for Alaska on her single sideband radio out of Kodiak with her call sign WBH29 since before I took my first King crab trip aboard the *Miss Donna* 18 years before. Over the years, her voice became as much a part of the Alaska maritime industry as the winds and the waves that she forecast, the radio chatter diminishing to abrupt silence when she signed on each morning and evening to give the day's forecast. This was a daily ritual for thousands of fishermen from the Aleutian Islands to Southeast Alaska to tune in to find out what the coming weather had in store for them. Whether Peggy knew them or not, many felt that they knew her and were grateful for the sense of community she brought to the fishing boats and tugs that plied the cold waters of the north.

I was not one to listen to the weather much when fishing offshore; if the weather was good I knew it, and if it was bad, I knew that as well. And when the weather was bad, we had nowhere to hide anyway. The *Ballad* was a tough boat when it came to the weather, and while the ride might be miserable, she was capable of riding out most of the weather that swept across the northern waters from May through September. But, she was no match for the vicious storms and mountainous seas that screamed across the Bering Sea and Gulf during the cold winter months, the snow blowing sideways and sea spray freezing upon contact until the large crabbers and draggers chasing Opilio crab, Pollock and cod came to resemble boat-shaped icebergs. At times like that, the crews would spend hours with sledgehammers and baseball bats breaking the ice up and shoveling it over the side before its weight endangered the boat's stability. The work was backbreaking, and I had had my share of it in years past. And while the winds and seas that hammered the West Coast could hold there own with what the Alaskan waters dished out, I was always grateful to get away from the relentless, unforgiving and bone-chilling cold.

"Area Five Bravo, Castle Cape to Cape Sarichef," Peggy announced as I turned up the radio, "Gale warnings. Northwest winds to 45 knots with higher gusts out of bays and passes. Seas to 15 feet. Rain. Outlook, northwest winds 35 knots."

"Great," I muttered to myself sarcastically. After two weeks of beautiful, sunny weather, the wind machine was turned on at last. The prevailing winds during the summer months were usually out of the southeast or southwest. When the winds shifted to the northwest with the coming fall, winter storms would soon be on their way, and it was my signal to go home. When that door slammed shut, it usually did so suddenly and violently.

Sea Spouts and Williwaws

A loud rumbling and rattling shook the *Ballad* as a gust of wind slammed into the starboard side, heeling her hard over. Looking toward the back, the entire top of the shelter deck was bowing upward as the wind did its best to tear loose the bolts anchoring it to the deck. Beyond, the air was filled with the smoky haze of sea spray whipping across the water's surface with the faint shadow of Cape Pankof 10 miles astern, looking like an old, washed out painting left out in the sun too long. Ahead, the golden glow from the lights of two, nameless vessels faded in and out like lonely sentinels that jogged back and forth in the lee of the island. We were just 12 hours from Dutch Harbor—12 hours from a secure berth and a hot meal. We would no longer have to worry if the shelter deck was going to blow off. We were 12 hours too late.

Between us lay Unimak Pass where we would cross over from the Pacific Ocean on the south side of the Aleutians to the Bering Sea on the north. The passes that separate the Aleutian Islands can be dangerous places with the tidal flow reaching 10 knots or more in places. I saw the tides turn six-foot seas into twelve-foot breakers, and that was during *good* weather. Boats far larger than the *Ballad* had their windows smashed out while crossing in bad weather. Unimak Pass was not one of the worst, but it was still impassable as the winds howled out of the northwest.

The weather arrived on schedule just as Peggy predicted, and we were forced to take shelter in the relative, although windblown safety, of Unimak Bight. The Bight was a long, smooth section of coastline stretching for some 30 miles along the south side of Unimak Island. Bowing slightly inward towards the north, it provided good shelter from the seas that pounded the other side of the island, but the winds were fierce. We jogged to the west until we ran out of island and could change course, steaming back to the east. The air pressure on the north side of the island would build as the winds slammed into the towering volcanoes making up the island, releasing itself in enormously powerful gusts that would scream southward through the valleys at 80 knots or more, creating massive williwaws, as they collided with the sea.

Looking up at the mountains, I remembered listening to David one winter as he described over the radio the glowing lava flows pouring down the mountain's flanks and how the mountain belched forth a towering cloud of smoke and ash. He had been Tanner crab fishing (before the crab stocks collapsed) on the opposite side of the island from where we were now jogging, and as I listened to him, I wasn't sure which excited him more: the volcano erupting or the fact that he was scooping up crabs, and only a few boats were around him.

"Whoa! Check it out!" I shouted in disbelief. Several miles ahead of us a column of water several hundred feet high was dancing and snaking its way across the water. The howling winds swept around the mountains and converged, intertwining themselves into a tight funnel that sucked up the seawater below, releasing it into a cloud of spray hundreds of feet in the air. I had never seen a waterspout before, and as I watched it, I wasn't sure I wanted to again—especially up close and personal. Williwaws were one thing, but the writhing, twisting column of water that briefly appeared was something else entirely.

"Whoo-hoo!" Chief called out as the towering funnel bent outward as the center of the column raced out to sea, leaving the rest to collapse in an explosion of snow-white spray that was quickly swept away in another gust of wind. With the show over, he adjusted the coffee-stained pillow behind his back and quickly shifted his focus back to the dog-eared copy of *Power Boat Magazine* with the resignation of a fisherman who has seen too many storms and no longer cares, so long as his boat is still safe.

The low rumbling and rattling began again, slowly building to a crescendo that shook the boat from stem to stern, providing the bass portion to the howling symphony being played in the *Ballad's* rigging by the wind. On our present course, we were broadside to the maelstrom with no mountain valleys to relieve the pressure. Although the shelter deck covered the entire back deck, as each williwaw slammed into the boat, the winds would rush in through the forward opening where the gear was brought aboard, and the air pressure would begin to build again. Only this time, it was threatening to tear the entire shelter deck from the bolts that held it fast to the deck, beating against the top-hatches and tub racks, looking for relief. I could see the entire roof bulging up some two feet as it rattled and shook with the wind's ferocity.

"Chief, go get Curtis to help you tie open the hatches on top of the shelter deck will ya?" I asked as Troy looked up from his magazine. "We've gotta find a way to let some of that air pressure out, or the wind's gonna blow it clear off the deck and all the gear with it."

"Yeah, okay," he responded, putting his magazine carefully aside and getting up from his seat on the port side of the wheelhouse. "If that happened, we'd be instantly rigged for crab. Only with no gear and no season—we'd be outta business."

"Yeah, how'd we explain that to David?" I asked with a laugh. "I'll swing around and point 'er into it so you guys don't get blown away. Be careful when you swing those hatches open, though, as they're gonna want to catch the wind when you swing 'em open."

"No sweat, Smitty," Troy replied as he slid down the wheelhouse stairs to the galley below with one final look at the gleaming, white yacht he was admiring moments before.

Twenty minutes later things were back to normal. Securing the hatches open seemed to be working as the rumbling and rattling was reduced considerably. Curtis was back in his bunk racing against time with the United Space Alliance as they attempted to thwart another invasion by the dreaded Cyborgs of Termilan III in the Gamma Sector. Chief was once again sailing the warm waters of the Caribbean with a boat full of bikini-clad women. Marty was asleep in his bunk surrounded by the odd collection of clothes, tools, books and fishing gear that so often left little room for Marty himself. Turning the boat around to steam back towards the east end of the Bight, I groaned as I settled back into my chair. I hated stopping. And stopped we would be for at least another 12 hours before the diminishing winds and favorable tides would make Unimak Pass once again fit for passage.

Red Sky in Morning, Sailors Take Warning

"Let 'er go!" I announced over the loudhailer, the command echoing through the dark spaces beneath the fuel dock as it bounced between the black, slime-covered pilings. I walked out the wheelhouse door and looked over the starboard rail. I watched the stern line splash into the water and slide its way around the piling that held it fast before disappearing into the stern chock like an enormous, brown snake burrowing into a hole. Ahead of me, Curtis gave a quick flip to the bowline, shaking it free of the bollard up on the dock to swing down and bang against the hull. He then hauled it aboard in big coils, bent over and picked it up to carry it aft of the wheelhouse where he would tie it in place.

"Weather doesn't sound too good," he commented in his classic, understated sort of way as he made his way aft. Curtis had always been like that, understated and mellow. He was an excellent crewman, nonetheless, and if I walked off the boat, he could have taken over and the whole operation would not have missed a beat.

"Nope," I replied, with an equal understatement, "It certainly does not. But if we make tracks, hopefully we won't get our asses kicked too badly."

After jogging for 12 hours in Unimak Bight, we finally made it across the pass and on into Dutch Harbor. Although the wind diminished substantially, more of the same had been forecast, so instead of getting beat up out by the Four Mountains, I decided to fish in Beaver Inlet. Just four hours from Dutch on the east end of Unalaska Island, the inlet offered protection from the wind driven seas as another gale swept through the very next day.

Beaver Inlet traditionally produced good fishing for us, but during the last couple of years, it seemed to slow down considerably. Nevertheless, the thought of getting beat up by the seas and losing more gear out at the Four Mountains (if the weather allowed us to fish at all), had been less than appealing, so I gambled on Beaver Inlet. Thankfully, my gamble paid off. The wind howled through the narrow pass to the immediate north that separated Unalaska and Unalga Islands, but the islands themselves blocked the stormy seas that battered their northern coasts.

Although nothing to write home about, the fishing was steady, and after 48 long hours of fishing, we caught the last of our fish. With the wind coming down once again, we pounded our way through Unalga Pass and around the corner to Dutch Harbor in time to catch a cab over to Stormy's for a piping hot dinner followed by a restful night's sleep tied to the Westward Seafood's dock over in Captain's Bay.

Highliners Expect Success

The next morning, we top-iced the fish holds, packing any air spaces with the freezing flakes that shot out of the 10" ice-machine hose at 100 mph, leaving just enough room to secure the hatches before steaming back around the corner to the Petrol Marine fuel dock to top off our tanks and grub up at the AC store down the road. I was anxious to "make tracks" as another low was beginning to work its way down the Aleutian chain with still another sliding over from Siberia, hot on its heels.

"Area 12 Alpha," Peggy's voice came through loud and clear as we made the corner and started to pick up speed, the outgoing tide sweeping us into Unalga Pass. "Small craft advisory. Southeast winds 20 knots, switching to southwest 20 by this evening. Seas eight feet. Areas of fog. Outlook southwest winds 35 knots." This wasn't a bad weather forecast, but with the size of the low heading our direction, I didn't want to be anywhere near "Area Twelve Alpha" in the coming days. We had a boatload of fish, 2,000 miles of North Pacific Ocean between us and a scheduled offload in Bellingham, Washington. If we were stuck waiting out another storm behind an island somewhere, our fish would be too old after a seven-day crossing to be sold on the fresh market—maybe even too old for the freezers. The last thing I wanted was to be forced to sell in Alaska and bring an empty boat south. Besides, I reasoned, the storm track at that time of year typically carried the low-pressure systems along the Alaska Peninsula before dipping below Kodiak where the lows would either eventually blow themselves out somewhere in the Gulf of Alaska or come ashore in Southeast Alaska. Then again, this was not a typical year.

Over the Horizon

"What's on the menu for dinner, Marty?" I asked as I sat lounging in my chair with my feet up on the dash. This was the only position I could find that was even remotely comfortable. The Captain's chair in the *Ballad* was made from a heavy, metal frame with a heavy, brown, wool cover stretched over cheap foam padding. The seat was too short to support my legs, and the straight back dug into my spine. I was sure it was recovered from a medieval torture chamber someplace where prisoners were forced to sit in it for hours on end while a wicked-looking guard shouted "Sign zee papers!" in their face. David figured it kept people from falling asleep while on watch, but I was not so sure. I ran the Bering Sea crabber *Aleutian Ballad* for a short time some years before, and the full-size, comfortable Captain's chair on that boat helped me to stay awake instead of zapping my energy like the one on the *Ballad*. Several years later, someone did fall asleep in that life-size, comfortable chair and ran into an island. No need to curl up at the galley table as Willie did on that one. No sir. So, with some resignation that perhaps it was for the best, I shifted myself in the chair as I eyeballed Marty standing next to me.

"How 'bout chicken?" He asked with a grin, his unwashed hair sticking out at impossibly crazy angles. Whenever we left port, Marty made sure we had at least one chicken in the freezer. He called them "storm birds" after a superstition he picked up somewhere that cooking a chicken would bring on a storm. And, I'll be darned if it *didn't* start to blow whenever he cooked one of those birds. I never paid much attention to seafarer's superstitions… usually. I heard so many of them over the years that apparently the only safe day to leave port was the second double-Tuesday following the third new moon in a leap year!

The widest held superstition among the fishing fleet was that leaving town on a Friday would bring bad luck. Sure enough, at 12:01 a.m. on a Saturday morning, boats would begin streaming out of the harbor. For most of my career, I followed along as more of an excuse to catch a movie or otherwise stay in town a bit longer than any fears of misfortune. As a matter of fact, I made some of my best trips after leaving on a Friday, although my crew was not pleased upon departure.

"The mind can convince a competent person that he is incompetent or an inadequate person that he is highly talented. Unfortunately, self-doubt and negative attitudes seem to have a more powerful influence on the mind than positive attitudes. Usually a person is not aware that he is setting himself up or limiting his capabilities."

- Bruce Bowman -

"Go ahead and cook the bird, Marty," I said, calling his bluff as he stood waiting for my answer. We had this exchange many times before, and my answer was always the same.

"No way, Boss. You want it to start blowing?" he asked, giving me a look of admonition.

"The winds seem to blow anyway," I replied with a laugh. "But since we're racing a storm, how 'bout pork chops?"

"You got it!" he smiled "What's Peggy have to say anyway?"

"I dunno. I suppose we should find out, huh?" I said as I reached for the volume control on the radio where we could hear Peggy's forecasts, starting with Southeast Alaska and moving her way westward. We were 24 hours out of Dutch and nearly 150 miles offshore. The weather swung around to the southwest earlier in the day as forecast, but it hadn't blown much over 20 knots and diminished to just a light breeze since then.

"Area Twelve Alpha," Peggy's voice came in loud and clear, "Storm warnings. Repeat, storm warnings. Northwest winds 80 knots. Seas 23 feet. Rain. Outlook northwest winds 60 knots."

Marty and I looked at each other, the good humor that permeated the wheelhouse just moments before evaporated. "Hope it doesn't head this way," Marty commented in an understatement that rivaled Curtis at his best. "I'm keeping that bird in the freezer for sure." With a full load of fish and our fuel tanks topped off, we were heavy in the water with less than a foot of freeboard separating the main deck from the water's surface. Loaded as she was, 80-knot winds would invite very serious trouble as the Ballad would be pushed to the very limits of her seaworthiness and perhaps beyond.

"Get the rest of the guys up and make sure everything on deck is secured." I told Marty. "Move as much stuff forward as you can, and make sure everything that can move is tied down."

"You got it, Boss," he said as he turned and slid down the stairs to the galley calling out for Chief and Curtis.

I walked over to the chart table to mark our current position on the ragged chart pinned to the corkboard beneath. It was suffering from too many voyages with its once clean, white surface now covered with coffee stains, penciled-in course lines, smudges from position fixes that were erased over the years and a variety of other blotches from who knows what. I marked our position (just north of the course line) and returned to my seat, double-checking the rest of the navigational electronics as I did so. Looking out on the smooth, flat waters ahead of us, the ocean seemed to be taking in an enormous breath before blowing us over the horizon. An old sixties song started to run through my head as I gazed out the window, "Nowhere to run to baby, nowhere to hide…"

On the Edge

"A one-thousand-five millibar low, two hundred miles south of Montague

Island will move southeast and to 200 miles northwest of the Queen Charlotte Islands by Wednesday evening." Peggy's morning broadcast cut through the morning stillness. The low-pressure system that forced us to take shelter behind Unimak Island slid across the Alaska Peninsula and Kodiak Island and into the Gulf of Alaska. Now it was being pushed to the southwest, threatening to bring with it gale force winds to the seas ahead. While not strong enough to be threatening, it would surely bring strong southeast winds to the seas ahead of us. Her next announcement stopped me cold.

"A nine-seven-five millibar low 100 miles south of Cape Sarichef will move to 300 miles south of Kodiak Island by early Wednesday morning..." Continuing to listen intently, I walked over to the chart table, picked up the solid brass dividers that lay in the tray at the table's edge and stretched them across the latitude lines until the distance between their two points equaled 60 miles. Beginning at Castle Cape, I began walking them down the chart counting the miles as I went, but I already knew where they would stop. Sixty, 120, 180 and 240...the dividers landed almost directly on our course line some 50 miles ahead of us. The door was slamming, and it was slamming hard before we moved all the way through it.

I spent most of the previous evening listening to the radio as the fleet shared weather reports amongst themselves. The low-pressure system that was forecast to move through the area bringing gale force winds developed into an immense storm, packing winds of 80-100 knots and building mountainous seas as it battered the Peninsula mercilessly. All maritime transit along the western end of the Alaska Peninsula, clear out to Umnak Island 300 miles west, came to a grinding halt; the boats unable to reach port, wisely holing up wherever they could find cover in the bays and behind the islands that covered the area. But their weather would soon improve as the storm slipped off what would have been the usual storm track for September, moving instead to the southwest directly along the Ballad's course line that I drew two days earlier. Suddenly, we were 500 miles offshore and running for our lives at a breakneck speed of only 9.5 knots.

*"You gotta play the hand that's dealt you.
There may be pain in the hand, but you play it."*

~James Brady~

Still leaning on the chart table, I looked out the aft windows and examined the sea behind us. The slight northwesterly swell that joined us earlier in the day was framed by a line of angry, gray clouds looming far off on the horizon as the daylight faded, giving the sea a soft, muted look. Not even so much as a puff of wind marred the glassy waters. Behind the two totes of halibut gear tied to the forward rail of the shelter deck were the twelve orange marker flags nestled in their rack, hung limp in the still air, oblivious that on the far off horizon, a huge storm was bearing down on us.

After marking our position on the chart, I jabbed the dividers into the corkboard in frustration and walked outside to look over the side. After two days of running, burning 50 gallons of diesel fuel per hour, the boat was beginning to lighten, and I was glad to see the rub-rails were no longer dragging in the water. With one last glance off to the west, I returned to the wheelhouse and slumped into my chair, considering the weather forecast I just heard.

The huge storm that was chasing us across the North Pacific in and of itself was dangerous enough, but if it collided with the low moving down from the Gulf…I didn't even want to think about the consequences. It could very well be a "Perfect Storm" similar to the one that took the *Andrea Gail* down in 1991 and all the crew with her. Sliding out of my chair, I walked back over to the chart table and stood studying its ancient surface, considering my options. Unfortunately, I didn't have any. The only sure way to get out of the storm's path would be to adopt a more southerly course in an attempt to get out of its way, and doing so would add an extra 24 to 48 hours of running time to our crossing. The *Ballad's* limited fuel supply would not allow it, though. We made the crossing enough times that I knew upon arriving in Bellingham, we would have just 24 hours of fuel left in the tanks. My only option was to stay on course, hoping and praying that the storm either would blow itself out or change course to the north. What a kick in the pants, I thought. My last fishing adventure might end up truly being my last, and Lorraine would be a widow before we ever said, "I do."

Leaving the chart table, I returned once again to my chair with that old sixties song playing once again in my head, "Nowhere to run baby, nowhere to hide..."

Judgment Day

"Hey, Smitty," Chief called out, "It's almost eight o'clock."

"Yeah, okay," I responded. The crew finished backhauling the gear before we had been 12 hours out of Dutch, and with four days of running with nothing much to do but read and sleep, I was getting tired of bunk time. I rolled out of bed, stretching out the dull ache in my back before standing up to peer out the windows. The boat was still riding smoothly, and as I stood up, I still half expected to see the wind whipping across the sea. Instead, I was greeted with the same, glossy, slate-gray sea that had been with us since our second day at sea. The following swell gradually increased and was now at eight feet, a foretelling of the fury behind us. But as each swell passed under the boat, passing from stern to bow, it helped to push us along.

The previous day, our course finally took us out of the Alaska Current, a great river of water that swept westward along the Alaskan Peninsula. No longer bucking against the current and with a following sea, we picked up nearly a knot and a half in speed and were now averaging nearly 11 knots. Reaching past Chief, I turned up the radio as Peggy began her Wednesday morning broadcast.

"A one-thousand millibar low, 400 miles northwest of the Queen Charlotte Islands will move to 100 miles west of the Queen Charlottes and become stationary by late Thursday evening." This was still not good news. "A nine-eight-zero millibar low, 250 miles south of Castle Cape will move to 400 miles southeast of Kodiak Island and intensify to nine-seven-zero millibars."

Back at the chart table, I picked up the dividers and began walking them across the chart once again. The low slowed a bit, but it was still moving down our course line, ever closer, like a lion stalking its prey. Checking the GPS, I marked our position on the chart, once again walking the dividers across the chart 60, 120, 180, 240 miles, along the course line ahead of us. From our current position 400 miles west of the Queen Charlotte Islands,

Thursday morning, God willing, we would be less than 200 miles from Cape Scott on the northwest tip of Vancouver Island—200 miles and 24 hours from a place to hide. If we could make it that far, I was confident that the storm would either blow itself out or change course to the east—or both.

> *"Talking about grievances merely adds to those grievances.*
> *Give recognition only to what you desire."*
>
> *- Thomas Dreier -*

"Today is judgment day," I thought, as I climbed into my chair and gazed out the windows at that glassy water reflecting the morning light off the swells passing beneath the boat. We had been racing across the sea riding a trough of calm weather ahead of the storm, and if we could continue to do so for another 24 hours, we just might squeak through the door before it completely slammed shut.

"We're gonna beat this sucker, Chief," I announced as I turned the radio down once Peggy's weather forecast was complete. He was busy converting my bunk into a seat, tossing my pillow and sleeping bag back, swinging the forward half of the bunk up and back to the latch along the wall and straightening the seat cushions.

"Woo-hoo!" he answered back as he reached over to the dash, picked up the barely recognizable copy of *Power Boat* magazine and let it fall open to the page with the gleaming, white, 50-foot Fountain. I laughed out loud as I watched him, amazed that he could spend so many, endless hours staring at the same boat.

"How can you look at that thing so much?" I asked, giving him a hard time.

"Whatcha' mean?" he replied.

"That boat! How can you stare at that yacht so much?"

"Ya' mean this one?" he asked, holding up the picture for me too see.

"Yeah, that one."

"I dunno, probably the same reason you always stare at this one," he answered, flipping ahead several pages before holding up the magazine again.

"Yeah, but that one's got a lot more deck space on top," I said, turning in my seat to face him. "Plus, the stern folds down, making it a good dive boat."

Chief examined the page for a moment and turned the magazine back to the original page he had open, pointing out the advantages in the sleek design. The morning hours soon passed on into the afternoon as we sat talking, the conversation drifting easily from boats to politics to fishing or whatever happened to come to mind. This became our daily routine, polished and perfected after too many days at sea.

As evening arrived, the smell of Marty's cooking began to waft up from the galley below, accompanied by the distorted sound of rock and roll turned up way too high that was beginning to give me a headache. After marking our position on the chart, I slipped out of my chair and slid down the wheelhouse stairs to the galley below.

"What's for dinner, Marty?"

"I'm cooking the bird, Boss," he replied.

"You're *what*?" I asked in amazement.

"I'm cooking the storm bird."

"Why? We've had a storm chasing us for the last thousand miles. You're tempting fate a bit aren't you, Buddy?" I asked with a wry grin.

"Nah, I'm feeling lucky today. Besides, we're almost out of food, and it's all I got left for dinner…unless you want some of this leftover stew again," he answered, shoving a crock-pot under my nose that was warming the same stew for the last three days. The edges were burned solid with the dried, brown surface broken into a myriad of interwoven cracks.

"Whoa, no thanks," I said, pushing the crock-pot away in disgust. "The bird'll do fine."

I looked suspiciously at the neat sections of chicken lying in a bed of vegetables and bubbling broth, noting that the pan was not even secured to the storm rails that bordered the burners of the stove. Turning around, I grabbed the rail on the stairs and scampered back up the steps to the wheelhouse, calling over my shoulder as I went, "I don't believe in that superstition stuff anyway! And turn down that music will ya? The weather's on!" Back up in the wheelhouse, I turned up the radio just as Peggy started her broadcast.

"A one thousand five millibar low, 200 miles northwest of the Queen Charlotte Islands will move inshore Thursday evening and begin to dissipate.

A nine-eight-zero millibar low, 300 miles southwest of Kodiak Island will move into the Gulf of Alaska by late Thursday and diminish to nine-nine-five millibars by Friday morning."

I heard a flutter of paper as Chief's copy of *Power Boat* landed on the dash next to my hand. It had been folded back to reveal a beautiful, 50-foot offshore powerboat with pink and green accents painted along its sides. "Smitty, ya' gotta admit that Fountain is really the way to go…" Chief began, his by-now-familiar admirations of the yacht in the picture fading into the background.

"If the winds of fortune are temporarily blowing against you,
remember that you can harness them and make them carry you
toward your definite purpose, through the use of your imagination."

~Napoleon Hill~

We raced a killer storm for over twelve hundred miles across the North Pacific, and as I reflected back on the last four days, I was struck by the strangeness of it all. The storm we took cover from behind Unimak Island, as the ones before it, moved across the Alaska Peninsula and into the Gulf before swinging south to come ashore in the Queen Charlotte Islands. A similar low-pressure system was now following a similar path. But the monster storm that chased us for so many miles took a different path. After racing across the Aleutians at 20 knots, it swung far to the south, moving almost directly along our course line. But in doing so, it slowed its advance, and as if some unseen hand delivered us from its ferocity, we made the crossing in fair winds and a following sea.

"…and besides," I heard Chief say, "If we had that Fountain, we could have made it across in just under two days." I smiled at the thought as I put my feet up on the dash, settled back in my chair and gazed out the window. Suddenly, I saw a flash of movement out of the corner of my eye.

"Hey, check it out! First one in days!" I said to Chief as I watched the lone Fulmar soaring above the waves ahead before banking up into a wide, sweeping turn to race by the boat once more.

CHAPTER TWENTY
Night Magic

"If the work of God could be comprehended by reason,
it would no longer be wonderful,
and faith would have no merit if reason provided proof."

~Pope Gregory I~

As we neared the southwest coast of Vancouver Island, I marveled at the beautiful evening. The wheelhouse doors were opened wide, and the fresh, night air moved through the cabin. Although dark, the outside temperature was still in the 70's, and the waters were calm. What a magical night without so much as a ripple to betray the mirror flat surface of the water. The sea seemed to melt into the dark night air in the golden-black glow from the big sodium lights mounted on the mast. With only the hum of the engines breaking the incredible stillness, the *Ballad* seemed to hold still in both space and time.

I heard steps on the wheelhouse stairs, and as I turned, I was greeted by a smile from Marty with a hot cup of coffee. "How's it going, Boss? What a beautiful night. Seen any meteors?" he asked, referring to the Perseids meteor showers that take place each summer.

Surprise!

"No, I forgot about them," I replied. "Let's go outside and check it out."

Marty always came up with great ideas. I reached over, flipped off the switches to the mast lights, and the *Ballad* was immediately plunged into blackness, punctuated only by the soft, green glow from the radar and the depth sounder. Picking up the binoculars from the dash, Marty and I made our way out the open doors alongside the wheelhouse and up to the bow. Standing in the warm night air, we stared up at the heavens, utterly transfixed. Out at sea far away from the glow of city lights with the boat running in darkness except for the red and green navigational lights, the sky overhead was a riot of stars, sparkling and twinkling in every color imaginable. Looking up into the heart of the Milky Way galaxy, the stars were so numerous they appeared almost as a haze.

"There's one!" Marty announced pointing to a streak of light in the sky as a meteor collided with the atmosphere far above. "There's another one!" Soon, the sky was full of shooting stars! Streaking across the heavens, sometimes in short bursts and sometimes nearly to the horizon, the Perseids put on a magnificent show, and we had front row seats.

Ten minutes later, still enjoying the night sky, I suddenly caught a flash of color out of the corner of my eye. Looking to my left, my heart stopped at the unmistakable phosphorescent wake of two torpedoes speeding towards the bow of the *Ballad*. "What's that?" I asked in alarm, rushing to the rail, pointing. With impact seconds away, all we could do was watch.

But just at the moment in time we should have felt an impact, the "torpedoes" turned 90-degrees to move with the direction of the boat. Looking down, I saw one of the most incredible sights I ever saw in my many years of fishing. Two dolphins were riding the pressure wave caused by the *Ballad* moving through the water, and as they swam, the pale green glow of the phosphorous in the water lit them up from nose to tail. As we watched them swim, it seemed as if we were watching green dolphins flying in space!

Lying on the deck with our heads hanging over the edge, we were hooting and hollering like schoolboys as the dolphins smiled up at us, keeping pace with the knife-edge of the bow slicing through the water. Suddenly, the blackness of the sea surrounding the dolphins exploded in green flashes and streaks shooting outward from the dolphins at the bow! "Yeah!" Marty yelled out, "Did you see that! What was it?"

"I dunno! Probably a school of salmon or something!" I laughed back, "This is incredible! We gotta let Chief and Curtis know about this. C'mon!"

With that, we jumped up and ran inside the wheelhouse, down the stairs and across the galley to burst into the crew's stateroom, breathless with excitement.

"You guys gotta check this out...star streaks...you wouldn't believe it... dolphins...it's incredible...they're green... and...!!" Curtis looked up from his book and Chief rolled over in his bunk to see what was going on with the two blathering idiots who suddenly appeared, arms waving this way and that in the middle of the previously quiet and peaceful stateroom. Marty and I, both grown men, veterans of the tough and dangerous Alaskan fishing industry, probably provided as much entertainment for Chief and Curtis as the dolphins did for us as they watched us acting like a couple of 8-year olds during their first trip to the county fair. "...explosions in the water...and... well, come on!" and suddenly we were gone, bolting out of the stateroom, back up the stairs and onto the bow.

With a new wife at home, my path was leading me in a new direction. That voyage, and indeed that night, was to be my last as full-time Captain of the *Ballad*. As Marty and I sat on the bow in the warm summer air watching the dolphins skimming below the stars, memories of hardship, storms and ice seemed to melt away. All seemed right with the world, and I thought maybe, just maybe, this magical night was my going away present. I couldn't wait to tell Lorraine about my send off at sea. I indeed had a great run, but a new chapter of life was beginning for me. I was looking forward to the new adventures we would have together as a couple.

CHAPTER TWENTY-ONE
New Beginnings

"If you have a dream, give it a chance to happen."

~ Richard M. deVos ~

The cloudless sky slowly turned from gray to pink and finally to a brilliant blue as the warm summer sun rose over the Cascade Mountains, its welcoming rays reaching out to us as we glided up to the unloading dock in Bellingham, Washington. Our arrival marked the end of my career, and I had a touch of sadness as I reached over to switch off the main engines for the last time, the heartbeat of the boat fading away into the morning. Yet, what had once drawn me to the most dangerous and deadliest occupation in the world was losing its foothold. A new life was calling me.

David was driving up from Oregon to take the *Ballad* back up the Inside Passage to make one last, albeit small, black cod trip outside of Dixon Entrance. After delivering the catch in Warrenton, Oregon, he would tie the boat up in her slip, where she would remain until crab season, after which she would set out to sea once again. He wanted to leave that evening, so I climbed up to the dock and set out in search of a pallet of bait. Chief and Curtis were busy, unbolting the hatches and clearing the deck as the unloading crew gathered on the dock, arranging totes in long rows where the halibut would be sorted according to size.

I returned to the boat a half-hour later to see the unloading process in full swing. The crane operator lowered a heavy, nylon net 10-feet square into the fish hold. Chief and Curtis quickly unbuckled it from the cable, tossed it aside, gathered up the corners of the previous net and hooked them back on the cable before taking cover as yet another bulging bag of halibut emerged from the hatch, dripping long tendrils of slime. As soon as the loaded bag was clear, they quickly spread out the empty net and began tossing large fish into the center. I stood on the shelter deck watching them for a few moments before climbing back up on the dock and into the cannery to keep an eye on the weights being recorded.

As each bag of fish was brought up to the dock, it was dumped onto an aluminum table, the ice swept out of the body cavity, head chopped off and slid onto a scale before being tossed into a tote. As the fish were sorted, I would occasionally walk over to the totes of fish and poke them with a finger, checking for freshness. The meat was nice and firm to the touch, indicating that the fish made the seven-day journey quite nicely.

The $1.50 per pound price for our catch was disappointing, but I resigned myself to the reality of low prices several months earlier. "Oh well," I thought as I looked over the processing line, "That's just the way it goes sometimes." Over the last 18 years, I saw the same cycle repeated over and over again.

Supply and demand largely determined the price offered to the fishermen. Lower quotas meant higher prices as the competition between fish buyers increased while increasing quotas too often resulted in declining prices as we saw during the summer. The sad part was that regardless of the wild fluctuations in price, the consumers always seemed to be screwed in the end. The grocery store chains charged ten times what the fishermen were paid in an effort to recover their losses as unsold fish sat spoiling in the display case, while shoppers briefly looked them over before setting out in search of more reasonably priced meat.

As the morning faded away to the afternoon sun, the list of weights on the tally sheet grew from one row to three. Finally, the last fish was hoisted up to the dock, bringing our total weight to 54,000 pounds. Walking up to the cannery to sign the fish ticket, I could hear the clanging of metal bin boards and the rush of a hose as Chief and Curtis set about cleaning the hold and washing down the deck in preparation of taking on another 15 tons of ice for their last trip up north.

Returning to the boat twenty minutes later, David greeted me. "Hey,

Smitty!" he said with a smile as he stepped down off the rail at the edge of the dock to shake my hand, "You sure you don't want to go on this last trip?"

"I'm sure" I replied with a wry smile. "I got married in June and went back up to Alaska two weeks later. I've been married four months now and haven't seen my bride since our honeymoon!"

"Yeah, I know. Well, we're going to head out this afternoon, so let me know if you change your mind. Hey, Chief! How much bait did you guys get?" he hollered down to the boat as he started down the ladder.

David was not one to dwell on the past. He could not afford to. With an uncanny ability to produce results, he was always looking ahead, all the while juggling numerous irons in the fires of opportunity. Wasting time worrying about what *could* have been was a good way to be burned. I watched him as he walked out on the shelter deck, joking with the crew as they loaded the bait freezer full of boxes of frozen squid. I worked for David for 12 years, and while it was exceedingly frustrating at times, he became both a mentor and a valued friend. I would miss working with him.

Departure time came two hours later, and Marty, Curtis and Chief all came up to the dock to shake my hand, thanking me for the good times and wishing me a bright future. With a lump in my throat, I waved goodbye to my friends as they pulled away from the dock, a long chapter in my life coming to a close. I stood on the dock watching the *Ballad* making her way across Bellingham Bay bound once again for the cold waters of Alaska, and I was struck with how tiny she must appear upon the wide-open spaces of the sea. Bowing my head, I said a silent prayer for the safety of her crew and gave thanks for the time I spent aboard her.

The ocean, once in your blood, will forever call you. I'd been out at sea fishing most of my life; it was all I knew…up until now.

Standing in the gathering evening rays of the sun, the stillness of the evening carried a soft voice to my ears. "Hi, Sweetheart!" I turned to see Lorraine, my wife, my lover and my very best friend, standing behind me with outstretched arms. As we hugged each other tightly, the months apart melted away, and the frustrations of the summer began to disappear. Then we stood side-by-side, watching the *Ballad* slip out of sight as I told her of the many wonderful experiences and valuable lessons the sea offered me over the years. She slipped her arm around my waist and looked up at me with that incredible sparkle that is always in her eyes and said with a smile, "Why don't you write a book about it?"

"Maybe I will," I answered, "Maybe I will." As the last rays of the sun dipped below the horizon, we turned and walk away from the sea towards our new life together and an incredible date with destiny.

ABOUT THE AUTHOR

 Steve Smith spent 18 years of his life in the commercial fishing industry. During his time in the cold waters of the North Pacific, he worked his way up through the ranks to become Captain of one of the most successful Dungeness crab and long-line fishing boats in the fleet. In this high risk and ultra competitive industry, he honed his knowledge and skills in the area of leadership, teamwork, motivation and living life. He became a top producer and earned the title of Highliner, given only to an elite few out of a fleet of thousands.

In present day, Steve is a human performance professional consistently recognized for producing outstanding results in a wide variety of applications while maintaining high standards of integrity, business/client and staff satisfaction.

Steve lives in the Houston, Texas area with his wife, Lorraine. He still enjoys a great adventure through mountaineering, hiking, biking, rock climbing, surfing and skiing. To contact Steve for a *Lessons from the Sea* presentation, visit www.thetotalyou.biz for more information.